RACING DRIVER

RACING DRIVER

F1 Through a Driver's Eyes,
Heart and Soul

Norman Howell

A **RACING POST** COMPANY

DEDICATION
To Francesca and Tom

Published in 2007 by Highdown
an imprint of Raceform Ltd
Compton, Newbury, Berkshire, RG20 6NL

Raceform Ltd is a wholly owned subsidiary of Mirror Group Limited

A catalogue record for this book is available from the British Library.

ISBN 978-1-905156-22-1

Cover designed by Tracey Scarlett

Interiors designed by Fiona Pike

Printed in Great Britain by William Clowes Ltd, Beccles, Suffolk

CONTENTS

FOREWORD   6

INTRODUCTION   9

1   A VERY EXCLUSIVE CLUB   17

2   A BIG RIGHT FOOT   37

3   A BEAUTIFUL MIND   59

4   PAY DRIVER   85

5   MANAGING THE TALENT   105

6   FIT TO SIT   123

7   HE'S HAD A SHUNT   153

8   ANDY PRIAULX   169

9   TEAM BOSS   189

10 THE PRESIDENT ON DRIVERS   205

11 SNAPSHOTS   221

    CONCLUSION   247

    INDEX   252

FOREWORD

I am often asked about drivers, what's so special about them, why do they earn so much, why are they such big stars. I suppose I should know as I have been around them for more than 50 years. I was one myself, briefly. I have also managed them, found finance for them, looked after them in more ways I can remember. I also became friends with a few. That was in the old days, when sadly some of them didn't make a corner somewhere. It hurt when they never made it back to the pits and I suppose I then became less friendly and more business-like in my relationships.

It has been a privilege to have seen so many of them grow into wonderful and successful drivers, starting up as raw talent, unsure of themselves, each race improving, each race going faster, each time mastering their car, each Grand Prix making the best of what the team has put at their disposal. It's not easy, and there is so much to go wrong, even now that F1 is safer for drivers, and spectators. There is doubt, fear, pressure, a contract, a girlfriend, the media ... these matters, and many, many more can prey on a driver's mind, on his ability to be detached, cool, analytical.

Everyone who lines up on the grid on Sunday is a winner, every single one. It is their stage and everyone who is lucky enough to have access to the grid before the start of a race can feel the emotion, the adrenaline, the sheer focus pointing to each driver. The drivers have to perform. A matter of minutes after hundreds of people have been swarming over their cars and themselves, they are left alone. No more handshaking of princes and kings, of millionaires and billionaires, of rock stars and film stars. It's now them, their car, the first corner, the other cars.

FOREWORD

Money, celebrities and the global stage are what make F1 unique: it is the most glamorous sport because it has managed to retain its racing purity while delivering great value for some of the world's most important blue-chip companies. That racing purity is about what happens between when the lights go off and when the chequered flag is lowered in salute to each passing car and driver. Racing is the start and the finish of it all. There is nothing else that really matters. It's all about driving the car as fast as possible. Pure and simple.

This book goes some way to explaining the hugely complex make-up of a modern racing driver: readers who then watch a Grand Prix will get a clearer idea and a better feel for what it takes to line up on the grid. The simple answer is that it takes a lot, much more than the average person will ever have. Norman Howell has captured this, and much more besides, and I believe this is because though he has been around drivers for many years, he has also managed to keep a detached view of the goings-on in our sport. Detached but not lacking passion. His words celebrate the uniqueness of the racing driver in the sporting world.

Bernie Ecclestone
London, January 2007

INTRODUCTION

Being a racing driver is the coolest job of all. Most men have had the dream of being on the podium at Monaco, or Indianapolis, or Le Mans. It seems we all aspire to drive fast, to flirt with danger, to take a risk, to go to the limit. Then there's the glamour, the girls, the champagne, and the money – lots and lots of it. It's about Steve McQueen, James Hunt, Michael Schumacher and Juan Manuel Fangio. It's fact and fiction, like all the best daydreams. The lines are blurred, and in between these lines lies myth. Nations revere their national driver – Brazil for Senna, Germany for Schumacher, Britain for Mansell, Spain for Alonso – and they become mythical figures, hidden by their helmets, dominating their powerful machines with muscle and delicately steering them with pianist's fingers.

And it all seems fairly easy. It is dangerous, but probably no more so than tackling London's M25 or the Parisian Périphérique. At least on the circuits they're all professional drivers. There must be some skill involved, but not much that anyone can see from outside the car. Surely the engineers programme everything, the mechanics build it all, and the driver just gets in the car and drives as fast as he can for one and a half hours. I'll have some of that, I hear you say. And the girls too.

Well, not so fast – and no pun intended. It's actually very, very hard to be a racing driver. It takes many years to get to F1 (or Indy, or Nascar, or any of the other top motor racing series) – years of hard driving, of testing, of feeding gigabytes of info to the engineers, of analysing your own performance and that of the car. You have to start young and stay focused; you have to hang around grotty, cold, rainy and unforgiving circuits and garages, and some hot and humid ones too. Principally, you have to be quick. You also have to be careful or team owners will drop you: they can't afford smashed cars, especially in the early years. It's a business, and you must have the right people around you, to advise, to negotiate, to protect and guide you. You have to get on with people as you're only the most visible asset of a team. You get the glory but also the flak, and you get both big time. Race engineers don't mess about. You can't lie to them: the in-car data tell the true story. Where you took the corner wrong, where you lifted off the throttle – they know it all. And they've seen it all.

Drivers are complex characters. Loners, yet part of a team. And they must fulfil an ever-increasing schedule of media obligations and sponsor requests. They are mostly instinctive and reactive, yet they must plan and analyse the minutiae of their cars and driving styles. Glamour is all around them, so is temptation, yet the modern driver must lead an almost monastic life. They are under the media microscope, in a highly pressured environment. They are worth a lot, to a lot of people. And these people own chunks of them. Their time, their image, the best years of their life.

What goes on in their heads? How does it feel to race, to push the throttle and hit 200mph, then brake down to 60mph? How do they interact with the team owners, the media and the sponsors? How do they relax? Who are their friends? How do they feel after a race? Do they ever get scared? This book aims to answer some of these questions, insofar as these complex characters are linked by their love and mastery of speed, and separated only by DNA, culture, language and the availability, or lack of, money.

I am one of the lucky few with a season's pass, which gives me unrestricted access to the F1 paddock and to all the people who work hard, strut even harder and generally make up the strange, surreal, workaholic, brilliant and totally addictive world of F1. But I decided not to try to talk to just about everyone in the sport. I went instead for people who were experts in their areas, some in F1, others in other disciplines of motor racing. Crucially, they were all happy to speak freely – a precious thing in this sport, where some teams (in truth only one, maybe two) are still in the Dark Ages in terms of communication. There were more I could have spoken to, but the deadline hounds were after me.

It is usual to thank many people, and rightly so, as these writing endeavours would not be possible without the time and expertise given by all the people who know so much more than me about the subject of motor racing drivers. The sport's bosses, Max Mosley and Bernie Ecclestone, are quite extraordinary fellows, clear stand-outs in a pretty remarkable environment, much of it created by them. My thanks to them for, over the years, employing me, 'seconding' me, granting great interviews, sharing long nights at the Log Cabin, offering much-appreciated acts of kindness, and generally keeping me from needing to get a proper job for the past twenty years.

But my biggest professional thanks go to Jason Tomas, friend, football journalist and writer, who gave me the idea to write this book while partaking of some fine grilled kofte in a Turkish restaurant in London's Notting Hill. I was working in sports marketing at the time, not a natural berth for me, and was quite literally lost at sea, trying to get back into the writing game. Jason encouraged me to do just that and introduced me to Jonathan Taylor, who enthusiastically commissioned me to write this book. Two missed deadlines later, Jonathan must have regretted ever listening to Jason, but hopefully the final product, and the case of fine wine I sent his way, eased those jitters.

David Luxton is unquestionably the finest sportswriter's agent, ready to shoulder the burden of missed deadlines, a sharp negotiator with a true insider's knowledge of the book publishing industry. I sincerely hope he will stand in my corner on future projects. A case of wine on its way to you too, mate.

There are more to thank, of course. Sticking to the alphabetical so as not to upset anyone in the prickly paddock, I will start with ITV's James Allen, whose passion, knowledge and sheer *'joie de vivre en F1'* is matched only by his love for Liverpool FC, his family, and football coaching, though not necessarily in that order. Then there's Anne Bradshaw, PR lady to seven world champions; Flavio Briatore, truly a one-off and unique in his F1 achievements; Martin Brundle and Didier Coton, both managers, both from such different backgrounds; Frank Dernie, wonderfully quaint with his mug of tea, but razor sharp when it matters. E follows D, and in Mr E we have the Godfather of F1, a gentleman to whom all in the paddock owe a good living. His handshake is enough. Juan Manuel Fangio is not with us any more, but his legacy of grace under pressure is one the sport should never forget. Gary Harstein has followed in the footsteps of Professor Sid Watkins in establishing and maintaining high medical standards in F1, and both enjoy life to the full, with a twinkle in their eye. Johnny Herbert is a driver who has shown incredible resilience and good humour in the face of great adversity, while Joseph Leberer has looked after some of the greatest names in the sport, in body and in mind. Max Mosley has made huge contributions to driver and spectator safety, all the while keeping the team's senior engineers on their toes. Allan McNish has had a long and distinguished career at the very top of motor racing, as has Ian Phillips, who knows more juicy secrets than I've had hot meals. Andy Priaulx is surely the best driver never to have made the F1 grade, and a great pity it is, as the three-time touring car world champion would have made a great success of it. Money, or the lack of it, held him back.

Jo Ramirez was for many years the friendly face of McLaren, but he is of course much more than that: firstly, he is a gentleman; secondly, he is the bridge between the grand old days and the colder modern ones; and, thirdly, he once crazily asked me to deliver Ayrton Senna's Honda NSX back to Bruxelles airport. This was at Spa, and of course I took the beast and a colleague out for a spin on a wet and drizzly track. I was quite offended when said colleague insisted on getting out after only one lap. Anthony Rowlinson shared his deep and thoughtful knowledge of F1 over a long Brighton brunch. Sir Jackie Stewart is a great man who has made a lot of money out of the sport. And quite right too. The three-time world champion is still a central figure in the game: sharp, incisive, and with a lot to say on the subject of motor racing, always charming and willing to share his great knowledge. Mario Theissen, boss of BMW in F1, is another remarkably witty and very capable man, having forged an also-ran team into one of the main title contenders. Jacques Villeneuve has now left F1, and it is our loss, as his clear, impish intelligence and rebel-cool style lightened up some of the mostly dreary team briefings and press conferences. Mark Webber may be one of the very talented drivers who is too nice to become a world champion, but his Aussie fighting spirit and honesty shine through everything he does.

All the good bits are from these contributors. Any mistakes are mine, of course.

There are many others I did not interview formally but who over the years were kind enough to share many insights, scoops and glimpses of what being an F1 insider is all about. To them I owe a huge amount, in so many ways. From Italy, Pino Allievi of the *Gazzetta dello Sport*, the best F1 journalist in Italy, probably anywhere, a long-time friend, and truly a colleague; *Autosprint*'s Alberto Antonini, the second-best motor racing scribe in Italy, mad as a hatter, but always on the button; and Giorgio Piola, line-drawing maestro, who came to F1 via a show-jumping accident. From the UK there's Alan Henry and Maurice Hamilton, writing for the *Guardian* and the *Observer* respectively, both of whom I was reading while knee-high to a grasshopper. Like good wine, they keep improving, and one of the delights of my F1 season is to dine with them as they are deliciously indiscreet. Crispin Thruston and Eric Silbermann, snapper and scribbler respectively, have helped me more than I will ever be able to thank them for. And we had the wild times too. Marlboro's Nigel Wolheim took me under his wing when I first came into this game. He was press officer at Pirelli, and he steered me towards the best people in the paddock. His introductions were crucial to what success I have had in my writing. Peter Stayner never leaves a glass of wine empty in front of anyone and, just as important, he is one of the nicest fellows you could meet anywhere. Ron Dennis employed me, I fired myself, and in between I learnt much about management, problem-solving and how, if you scratch a bit under any human surface, there is gold to be had. Jean-Louis Moncet and Jacques Lafitte are wonderful and enthusiastic raconteurs from the bad, great old days of the sport. Always off the record. Formula One Management's Pasquale Lattuneddu, in charge of the organisation of all the races, and the FIA's media supremo Richard Woods have always been most gracious in lending a helping hand when one was needed, and did so with great discretion at all times.

I must also thank all the staff at the *Red Bulletin*, a mad but highly professional crew of very hard-working and talented journalists and designers, creative and extremely patient IT geniuses, stunningly efficient truckies and truly charmingly deranged printers. Pirates of the Caribbean each one of them.

It is a privilege to serve with them as we go raiding hither and yonder on the F1 circuit.

Finally, a special mention to Kate Robson, who very patiently and accurately transcribed most of the interviews, and to Matt Youson, who helped me out greatly on the 'Sit to Fit' chapter.

I'm quite sure I have forgotten many who have helped me at various times and, the F1 paddock being what it is, I will be reminded of this within minutes of arriving at the 2007 season's first race. Apologies in advance.

Lastly, a big thank you to Lalli, my wife and friend for 25 years who did my career prospects a world of good when, during what had been until then a convivial dinner, she told Ferrari boss Piero Fusaro that she thought all Ferraris were vulgar cars, for vulgar people. Luckily, he left the company soon after. *Grazie*, for your wonderful, unquestioning and constant support.

CHAPTER ONE

A VERY EXCLUSIVE CLUB

Sir Jackie Stewart is in no doubt that racing drivers are special people, an elite fraternity numbering very few at any one time. 'There are hundreds of millions of people who drive cars,' he said. 'Of those, a few million have competition licences; of those, a few hundred thousand do it on a regular basis, and a few thousand make a living out of it. Some, a few hundred, make quite a good living driving sports and touring cars, single-seaters and so on. Twenty of these are Grand Prix drivers.' Simply and clearly put: twenty out of millions is a clear indication of the elite status of these people. And what Sir Jackie said next brought the issue even more into focus: 'Not all twenty in a given season are always the best drivers in the world, but almost every one of them has won their national titles in each of the categories in the formative classes of the sport to get considered for F1, and though occasionally one will come along with a little more money than a talented one, none are mugs. But of those twenty, only six of them are any good at any one time.'

Sir Jackie, three times a world champion himself, then paused and looked at me. 'Do you consider yourself to be a good journalist?' he asked. 'Are you in the world's top twenty?' Before I could mumble some noncommittal response, he continued, 'Out of those six there are usually only three extraordinary talents at any one time, and almost always there is only one genius. Imagine all the lawyers, accountants, bankers, plumbers or writers in the world, if you could ask them, "Are you in the twenty, are you in the six, are you in the three, are you the genius?"'

Muhammad Ali would be able to answer that, and of course all top sportsmen and women feel that they can get to the very top, but it is still a tough question. And Sir Jackie is just talking about what goes on on track. Drivers are complete sportsmen who also have to be finished, packaged brand representatives, media-friendly and super-fit. They are the tip of the iceberg for very large commercial operations. A modern F1 team – before the latest round of agreements with Formula One Management (FOM), which are projected to boost incomes by a factor of nearly two – operates on a budget of between £200 million and £300 million, and the driver is the leader. Flavio Briatore, boss of Renault F1, remarked that a driver is like the commercial director in a large corporation, in charge of selling the product. 'A driver must never think he is driving his car, but our car, the whole team's car,' he said. 'It is as if he has power of attorney over the whole team. And it is deserved. Of course he has to motivate the team, drive really well and so on, but he is also an integral part of the team. So you are looking for someone who can transfer all the work into a reality on track.' The weight of expectation on the driver's shoulders is therefore considerable. McLaren has about a thousand employees working in the glass and concrete splendour of the McLaren Technical Centre near Woking in south-east England; Ferrari has hundreds of employees, 60 million fans (and that's just in Italy – all experts, of course), and three daily national sports newspapers. So, no pressure there.

What is more, for the top teams especially but also for the less competitive, the drivers must convert all this huge investment into results, and media time and exposure. 'One of the big questions for many teams when they evaluate a driver,' Sir Jackie pointed out, 'is how good will he be at converting that capital investment into a benefit to that investor, sponsor, team owner.' To reinforce this point, two years ago BMW asked a London sports marketing company to evaluate potential drivers in the light of their marketing value. There is no doubt that David Coulthard is the kind of driver whose prowess with the media and the brand managers counts as much as his driving ability. This passage in the 18 May 2006 edition of *Autosport* is typical of the thinking inside the paddock. Quoting a 'source' at Red Bull Racing, the article explained why DC, as he is commonly known, was in no danger of losing his place to McLaren's Juan Pablo Montoya for the 2007 season: 'So long as David is still doing the business on Sunday afternoon, why change him? He's a great professional, still fully committed, he trains hard, his testing and feedback qualities are excellent, and he's a superb ambassador, very good at marketing and the PR side.' In the end, Montoya, a great talent but also moody and not the easiest of drivers to wheel out in front of a few dozen corporate VIPs, decamped to the no-frills world of Nascar in the United States. DC remains at Red Bull Racing for 2007: charming, good-looking, with a stunning girlfriend (a former French TV presenter), the darling of the corporate world, at ease with the media and highly valued by his race engineers and team principal. Nearly the complete package. If the car were a little more competitive, he would be close to notching up the perfect score.

Being good with the media is crucial. During a race weekend many drivers will give between ten and twenty interviews during press conferences for the F1 print and radio media, separate television engagements and a string of sponsor-led commitments. And these are the regular, fixed interviews at each race. Depending on the fame of the driver and which country the GP circus has landed in, there will also be a raft of one-on-one requests and some straightforward Q&As, and variations on the theme, such as mini-sketches (Japanese networks are fond of these) and stream-of-consciousness 'downloads' of a lap for a local radio station. I saw, and heard, Jacques Villeneuve do this in French for Radio Montecarlo in 2006 – a true piece of bravura, as every bump, wrinkle and corrugation in the asphalt texture, every glint of the sun off the surrounding buildings was brought into his description. A few minutes before this, he was talking in Italian to a group of Italian journalists who were yet again (for the millionth time?) asking him about his father Gilles, an adopted national hero of Italy if ever there was one. Immediately after that he turned to me, smiled, shook my hand firmly, and answered my questions – in English, of course – about skiing, his forthcoming music album, the sense he has of danger, and what he would like to do after he stops racing. Courteous to a fault, always keeping eye contact with the interviewer, always focused on the next question. When I stood up, my time with him at an end, he had already turned his attention to another TV crew, from Germany, listening intently to their needs.

It's a tour de force repeated by all drivers during race weekends, at test sessions and at sponsor events all over the world. Some are more gracious than others – Jacques, like DC, was one of the very best – but all have to do the media work. There is no get-out clause. And that is a lot more than is asked of footballers, most of whom do not utter a word to the press on a normal Premiership or Serie A match day. Racing drivers must always be conscious of the brands they represent, which can be as disparate as tyre producers, oil suppliers, mobile telephones, insurance services, drinks companies and high-street banks. There are traps everywhere and becoming too familiar with some reporters can lead to big falls, so they are always on their guard. Their words are then reported worldwide, for motor racing is a global sport. What Fernando Alonso says is of interest not just to his Spanish fans; men and women (not to mention corporate PR and brand managers) in all the countries that host Grands Prix – sixteen of them in 2006 – and perhaps beyond that, will be eager to read his every word. That is a lot of people. No footballer is under that kind of scrutiny.

Mark Webber is among the most affable, cogent and professional drivers in F1. The Australian is also one of the more approachable people in the paddock and his many,

many hours of media work have left him in no doubt about what being in this very exclusive club is all about. 'If you really speak your mind, that can be dangerous for yourself, your team and sponsors,' he said, 'but if you toe the party line, then you come over as very dull. If I have to really express myself, I'd rather devote time and space to an interview. But that is not always possible. The escalation of media time is crazy. We have obligatory press conferences when we arrive at the circuit, then at the end of each session; plus there is the Paddock Club and all kinds of sponsor demands. In addition, we do print, radio and TV interviews. It just does not happen in other sports, not to this extent. But of course a driver is a very powerful tool in media and marketing terms. It can't all be about engines and tyres. Honesty is important, and I hate making excuses, like the wind changes direction. I really would like to be more outspoken.'

As Webber pointed out, in addition to being obliged to feed the media frenzy, at every Grand Prix drivers' attendance is required at the Paddock Club, a VIP hospitality enclosure hired by each sponsor at vast expense to house a daily guest tally of 300 to 400. The Q&A sessions are demanding as the VIPs often ask annoyingly inane questions or thoroughly indiscreet ones. Patience and courtesy are required, maybe just a couple of hours before a race, when a driver would rather be focusing on his start strategy, for example. All this every two weeks, plus test sessions and other sponsor-induced appearances.

Ron Dennis, McLaren's team principal, is notoriously very protective of his drivers, always reluctant to let them grant one-on-one time to the media. As far as he is concerned, they are in his team to drive, not to help journalists write stories. In turn the media hit back by being lukewarm about McLaren whenever they can, and this spills over to the drivers. When they were together at McLaren between 2003 and 2006, Kimi Raikkonen and Juan Pablo Montoya did not get a good press: the slightest escapade, on and off the track, was highlighted (and for both there was more than one), and that in turn did not please the sponsors. It's a vicious circle, and hard to break.

So there you have it, an identikit for the modern racing driver. If you consider all the skills required to be the best motor racer in the world – great at driving, excellent at processing disparate data, a natural media man (preferably in at least two languages), a team player, as well as good at public speaking and selling the brand image of your sponsors – it's an unusual blend to have to fit into a focused, driven, ego-centred individual. Not all will or can tick all the boxes, and some teams, but by no means all, help them out. After all, unlike in the old days when many of the drivers were so-called 'gentlemen' – which implied at least some knowledge of the ways of the world – many today have known only karting and single-seat formulae since the age of four or five. Their social skills are barely adequate for a fleeting appearance on *Big Brother*. Sir Jackie Stewart, for one, understood the importance of presentation. 'At Paul Stewart Racing,' he said, 'which my son and I did together, we sent all of our drivers to public-speaking courses, which included television appearances because they'd never seen themselves on TV. They were told not to pick their nose while on television, but also: don't look down, don't put your tongue out, make sure your tie's done up – and, by the way, can you tie a tie? And then you had to dress them, in everything, from shoes to socks to trousers and the blazer or the suit, so they learnt how to present themselves well.'

And the reason is sponsors, who are in motor racing because the sport is on television every other week during the season, all over the world – and drivers are the most sought-after piece of 'real estate' for the sponsor. The drivers know this well: it was taught to them and learnt by them as they came up through the lower formulae. Even as little kids in karting they would have been told, 'Be nice to your sponsor and don't forget to go and see him, whether he's the local florist, the funeral director or the laundryman. And, by the way, we need more than one sponsor, so go and be nice to a few more people as well.' The sponsorship requirements of the third-largest manufacturing industry in the world, the automotive industry, whose sharp end of technology is motor sport, are huge, partly because right from day one these sportsmen have totally different needs from anyone starting out in tennis, boxing, athletics, rugby and so on. From an early age you can go out and get a bucket of balls to play tennis or golf with, and get on the fairway, or find a wall or an open field. A driver, no matter how young he is, needs fuel, oil, chassis, tyres and mechanical know-how. And the learning curve can be a lot harsher: when young Tiger Woods was on a driving range and he sliced his tee-shot into the net protecting the public road, no big deal; but when little Lewis

Hamilton made the same degree of mistake in a little racing car by hitting a couple of walls on corners, his chassis might be damaged and certainly the wheels and tyres were destroyed. Money has to be found for the repairs. 'In this sense,' said Sir Jackie, 'motor racing is a unique cocktail of complex skills.'

And an expensive cocktail it is too, in so many ways. Take, for example, the salaries paid to the top drivers. The recently retired Michael Schumacher was neck and neck with Tiger Woods for top place on the *Forbes* Top Ten Sports Rich List for 2006, both listed as earning $80 million. The next European is David Beckham, in eighth place with $28 million. If we stick to motor racing, then Schumacher soars ahead: his nearest rival, American driver Dale Earnhardt Jr, came in at $20 million, and Michael's brother Ralf was in fourth with $16 million. Bernie Ecclestone, the man who has for many years controlled the commercial rights of the sport, is listed as the world's 200th richest man; in Europe, the *Sunday Times* Rich List ranks him just below the Peugeot family, at position 78, worth £2.3 billion; and he is listed thirteenth in the UK. And he is not the only one there from the world of motor racing. Ecclestone's long-time business partner Paddy McNally is the 146th richest man in Britain with £450 million – richer than Her Majesty the Queen, who is in 192nd place. Eddie Irvine, the former Ferrari driver, is in 357th place, Ron Dennis of McLaren is at 648, Dave Richards, the former British American Racing (BAR) principal and the front man for a new F1 team for 2008, is 858th, and Sir Frank Williams puts in an appearance at 878. The only other rich sports-related people are former Manchester United chairman Martin Edwards, and David Beckham, both from the world of football.

Some drivers come from money – to take karting seriously is an expensive commitment. In 2006 there was a young British driver in Formula BMW whose upper-middle-class parents from Surrey's stockbroker belt were down to their last remortgage and had gone as far as they could in terms of pouring money into karts and junior single-seaters to support their son. Lewis Hamilton has given interviews detailing how his father, by no means a rich man, had a number of jobs on the go, including – as the *Guardian* revealed on 23 May 2006 – putting up For Sale signs at £15 a go. Once Hamilton had shown that promise could be translated into results, McLaren took over much of his funding. In November 2006 it was announced that, for the 2007 F1 season, he would be driving for the team alongside world champion Fernando Alonso. But this is unusual in motor racing, where F1 teams' horizon is the next race; if there is any monitoring of young talent, it is limited to the GP2 races that take place on Grand Prix weekends.

There is very little mentoring or coaching as drivers are expected to use winter testing to familiarise themselves with a new car and team, or, if they stay in the same team, to adapt to the changes made to the previous year's car. And those differences can be huge, as tyres, electronics, fuel and aerodynamics can all make appreciable alterations to the way a car performs, as can the input from engineers as data and driver feedback is interpreted differently. So drivers don't get much time to impress new teams, especially if they are the third drivers. Like anyone who has made the step up from club football or rugby will tell you, 'When you play your first international match, everything seems so much faster and edgier. You focus so much to stay with the new pace that you don't have much recall later on.' It is very much the same in F1, as the unlucky Japanese driver Yuji Ide discovered to his cost in 2006 when he lost his seat with the Aguri Suzuki team following a series of catastrophic drives that culminated in the Fédération International de l'Automobile (FIA), the sport's governing body, requesting his immediate demotion.

In an interview with Japan's *F1 Racing* magazine, team principal and former Grand Prix driver Aguri Suzuki gave an interesting insight on why F1 was such a struggle for his driver. 'He didn't know the circuits,' he said. 'He'd run just 200 kilometres [125 miles] in an F1 car before Bahrain – that was tough. He didn't know how to drive an F1 car. He didn't know how to load up the tyres.' And, quite amazingly, 'He doesn't speak English. On the pit-to-car radio I had to translate. That was very awkward for him and his race engineer. In the practice sessions on Friday and Saturday I had to ask, "Yuji, what do you need now?" And because he's so inexperienced in F1, even I found his answers, given in Japanese, hard to understand.' Ide had come from the Japanese Formula Nippon Series, where he finished second in 2005 – a good result in a tough testing ground, but still clearly leaving him a long way from what is required skill-wise in F1. The FIA's decision was deemed harsh by many commentators, as the finger should have been pointed at those who gave him the super licence, without which you cannot drive in F1, and then those who employed him.

There have, of course, been plenty of other drivers who were quite a hazard for their fellow competitors, though they gave the fans their money's worth. Chief among them was Andrea De Cesaris, unkindly renamed De Crasharis by James Hunt. Paddock talk in 1981, his second season in F1, had it that he was causing so much damage to his cars that his mechanics were refusing to repair them. That year, in fourteen races, he crashed or spun off seven times. In his 208 Grands Prix, De Cesaris crashed twelve times on the opening lap of a race. In total there were 41 retirements through forced or unforced errors, and in all he retired 137 times, which is roughly two thirds of all the races he competed in. In the fourteen years he raced F1 cars – through family connections he stayed a Marlboro driver for most of that time – the Roman provided plenty of copy for the F1 media.

Like Sir Jackie, Didier Coton works in F1. His background and experience are very different from the Scotsman's, but in many ways they are in agreement on what makes a good motor racer. Finding young drivers is Coton's job; finding then managing them. He was mentored by Keke Rosberg in the role, and managed Mika Hakkinen to two world championships. The Belgian now has under his wing five drivers in various formulae. It is a measure of his success that the Finnish world champion has recently asked Coton to manage him once more, now that he has come out of retirement and is taking part in the German Deutschen

Tourenwagen Masters (DTM) series. Coton too has no doubt that, as a manager, he is looking for a special person, 'a complete package'. 'There are only a certain number of F1 drivers in the world, the number of seats are limited, and for each one of them you have to be absolutely special; you have to be one of the best in every category. After they spot two or three who make the grade [for speed], they will look at his language skills, at how he presents himself, at his attitude. There are lots of other parameters to evaluate; the one who will be chosen is the one who has the complete package. That's why I try to help them and train them to be good in every category – not only in terms of speed, but in the press, marketing and promotional work they do, and also how to be a human being, a nice guy, not an arrogant so-and-so. If today a driver isn't capable of having such qualities, he might become a good driver, but never a top driver. Take a look at world champions from this era, like Mika Hakkinen, Michael Schumacher, Damon Hill and Jacques Villeneuve. All of them managed to work under pressure; they could be fast; they had their way of recharging their batteries off the circuit; they did brilliant interviews; and they dealt perfectly with their promotions of companies, speaking well to CEOs of companies like they'd known them for a while. That's what I mean when I say it's a complete package.

'But,' Coton warned, 'one must never forget that a driver is a person before being a driver. This is very important, because a driver should be able to recharge his batteries without thinking about motor racing all the time. He needs to stop and enjoy life for the few hours and few days he has each month.' Coton is convinced that the ability to switch off is crucial as the demands are so intense, and so varied, that the constantly driven individual can easily grow stale mentally and physically, losing that small percentage of edge that makes the difference. Whether it's Fernando Alonso's card tricks, Michael Schumacher's football kickabouts or Mark Webber's work for his children's charity, something has to refresh, stimulate and relax beyond F1.

In many ways, motor racers, and F1 drivers in particular, can be seen as the most complete sportsmen in the world. Many of the required qualities have already been listed, yet there are others – fitness, analytical powers, courage – which will be looked at in the coming chapters. Yet there are still very many sports fans who struggle to see these drivers as extraordinary men. Perhaps this is because much of what they do is hidden from view: hands and fingers flying over the multi-task steering wheel, probing, pressing, pushing and pulling paddles, constantly adjusting dials and levers; then the legs, one pressing the brake, over and over again, at full, muscle-numbing loads, the other used as a brace for the rest of the body, helping to cope with G-forces up to five times the driver's body weight. The pain, the elation, the concentration … all is hidden behind the visor and under the helmet. Where is the grunt of the tennis player serving for the match, the sheer joy of a goalscorer, the brooding intensity of a front row as it is about to pack down, the other-worldly concentration that goes into a final putt at the eighteenth, the superhuman effort of the boxer who gets up after a knockdown? Many would have it that all this, and so much more, is 'real' sport. I have worked for sports editors who would routinely and scathingly ask when was I leaving for my next Grand Prix, 'to watch paint dry'. It's not a sport, more like a procession, others would say. Or, what kind of sport is this, where the rules are changed every year? And so on. There is, of course, much truth in these statements, and the world of F1 is guilty of navel-gazing of the most horrid and self-indulgent kind. It is also true that Frank Williams and Ron Dennis would race each other in wheelbarrows if one day their more expensive toys were taken from them. They are frighteningly competitive people, and they would soon be modifying the wheelbarrows to get some kind of advantage over their rivals. This is the nature of so many of the technical people in F1, including the drivers.

But there is another 'party' in the sport, one that is there to rival the techie one. Its agenda is entertainment, and the party leader is Flavio Briatore, who was given the cold shoulder when he first came into the sport but who is now the only team principal to have masterminded three successful world championships with two different drivers in two different teams, and on relatively small budgets. 'F1 is complicated,' he said, 'but I can assure you it is not as complicated as some people would have you believe. I have done many jobs which were harder than F1. Managing Benetton in the US, I can assure you, was much tougher. You know, producing a product without worrying too much about what the client thinks, as in F1, is easy. Ninety per cent of the people who watch F1 don't care about the technology. At Benetton, in the US, we had to produce what the end consumer wanted, or we would be in trouble. That is not the case in F1, as we all know. As far as I can see, this is a training ground for engineers, a gym for engineers. "I have invented this. Whether people like it or not, I don't care. We've invented this wonderful widget." Well, wow. Pretty soon the rest of the paddock will have it anyway. None of this is geared towards entertaining the fans. What are we ever doing for the fans, for the crowds at the races? I am convinced, and I have been since the days at Benetton F1, that we are spending crazy money, which makes no sense, and the client – the fan – has no idea why we spend all this money. If by spending this money we saw the quality of the show rise year on year, and saw more sponsors come in, well, then there would be some return on the investment. But that is not the case – on the contrary. We really need to take a hard look at ourselves. Let's put on a show to entertain people, let's promote young drivers, let's focus more on marketing and communication, let's work on our image, and within that of course there is a place for technology. We mustn't lose that, but let's put on a good show.'

That is what Briatore and the man he is very close to, Bernie Ecclestone, have been trying to do for a long time. The Italian feels that things began to move the right way in the early summer of 2005 with the entry of Red Bull into F1. 'When I look at Red Bull, it reminds me of the early days at Benetton, and this is the right way forward, to have many Red Bulls and the old Benetton, and Renault. But there are teams that keep going backwards because they appear to be fighting last stands all the time. This is entertainment, and the actors should smile every now and then. When a film is marketed, the actors make an effort and smile; here in F1 it always looks as if we've had a death in the family. In the old days we had the music and the models. We at Benetton kicked it all off, and because of that we were always regarded with suspicion, because maybe I wasn't born a mechanic. Strangely, though, some of these people hide their origins. Instead they should be proud that they were born mechanics and have become successful. They should be proud of their background and go out and have more fun.'

Making F1 more entertaining is also what the FIA, through its president Max Mosley, is trying to do, by tinkering with the rules in order to reduce costs and make the show a better one. But such is the concentration of extremely clever engineers in F1 that almost as soon as a new 'improving' rule is brought in, a means is found to nullify it. For his part, Ecclestone has been trying to unify the TV coverage, under the banner of FOMTV, so as to ensure a benchmark of quality, with clever digital innovations and the best viewing angles. But all this is lost on some of the die-hard techies, who care not a jot about entertainment. The ongoing tussle tends to belittle the extraordinary sporting achievements of the drivers and their teams.

Briatore is acutely aware that F1 drivers comprise a very exclusive club. When he was first asked by Luciano Benetton to run that company's team, in 1989, he told me then how amazed he was that such valuable commodities were not looked after, nurtured from a young age and generally commercially bound to teams for the length of their careers.

This is now happening as a number of young drivers are linked to teams and manufacturers. Renault, Red Bull, Toyota and Honda are very active in this area, while BMW has a single-seat formula car championship which it runs in Britain, Germany, the United States and the Asia/Middle East region.

Mario Theissen is the principal of the BMW F1 team, and his approach when it comes to drivers is straightforward – and in so many ways it sums up all that has gone before in this chapter. 'I follow a very simple philosophy,' he said. 'You can only market the best, so if you are not successful there is not much to market, and in terms of a driver, you need the best driver you can have – in terms of raw speed, racing intelligence, the ability to set up a car and to interact with the team, and physical fitness. So we have to get the best drivers on the market, then we have to get success, and then we can market that success.' BMW hope that their single-seater programme, Formula BMW – part of a broader racing programme which covers touring cars as well as F1 – will yield future racing stars. 'There are not many people who come over from touring cars to Formula One,' Theissen said. 'Some go the other way round, like Alex Zanardi, who is racing touring cars now for BMW. But it's Formula BMW that should be the natural breeding ground for future F1 drivers. Coming from karts they would do Formula BMW for one or two years then go to Formula Three, GP2 and F1. That's the area we are looking at when it comes to future drivers for formula racing. And it's almost worldwide now, and we support five F1 GPs with our series.'

But when it comes down to it, all those who are in the business of selecting, managing, paying and/or generally making a success of drivers know that there is only one true prerequisite for access to one of the most exclusive clubs in the world.

Speed.

CHAPTER TWO

A BIG RIGHT FOOT

'You can't teach them to be fast.' So said Ken Tyrrell, who in over 40 years in motor racing learnt a thing or two about what it takes to be a top driver (it was Tyrrell who signed up a young Scotsman by the name of Jackie Stewart and started him in top-flight motor racing). All team principals will tell you they would prefer to have a fast young driver. He might wreck cars, but he can be taught to drive better and within himself; raw speed you either have or you don't. It's in the genes, there's no doubt about it. Which is not to say that every driver's son will be as quick as his father, for there are so many other factors to take into account, such as the ability to manage a car, to interact with a team, to execute the right race strategy, to post fast laps, to know when and how to overtake, and how to win a psychological battle. But, without speed, all these other qualities are meaningless. In his early days at McLaren, some of the engineers felt that the young Mika Hakkinen did not have all the elements required to get to the very top, but all agreed he had a 'big right foot'.

Jo Ramirez has seen and lived with many of the top drivers since he came over to Europe from Mexico in 1961 to work with Ricardo Rodriguez, who raced a rented Ferrari at the Monza GP. Jo was at McLaren for many years, retiring in 2001. He was close to Ayrton Senna, and worked with pretty much everyone from Enzo Ferrari to Jackie Stewart, Ron Dennis to Ken Tyrrell. One of the sport's true gentlemen, he was, and is, loved and respected by all. And he too knows a lot about speed. Indeed, he had natural speed himself, as well as a fair amount of car craft, which he once demonstrated in Mexico City on the Thursday before a Grand Prix.

A number of McLaren personnel had dined downtown and were on their way back to the team hotel near the airport, quite some way away through dense traffic. Jo was at the wheel of an aged, wheezing and loaded VW Combi van, while the new test driver, a fresh-faced Finn by the name of Mika Hakkinen, was in a rented Ford saloon. One thing led to another and somehow things speeded up, with Jo and Mika racing for the hotel. In and out of the traffic they went, weaving and blasting the horn, eyeballing stunned and sometimes aggressive local drivers, accelerating through the tiniest of gaps, and braking hard with tyres squealing. Of course, the team principals were not involved. Though they have been known to have a little fun too at times, Ron Dennis would not have been too impressed had he seen the way in which Jo, by then in his 50s, carved up his hotshot new boy on the last turning into the hotel driveway, two wheels definitely off the ground, getting every bit of go-forward from the startled van, and leaving a red-faced Hakkinen to face the good humoured jeers of the mechanics and engineers when he finally made it to the hotel bar. The Finn, of course, went on to become world champion twice, and Jo retired quietly to Spain with his Harley-Davidson – a gift from Mika and David Coulthard. Both Ramirez and Hakkinen possessed natural speed. In this case, the older man's many years of experience of being a bit of a 'hooligan' in traffic carried the day, while the young Finn's reserve, in a new team in an unfamiliar city, blunted that extra edge he needed to win.

Young fast drivers always have an excess of wildness. That is the aspect that needs to be curbed to allow pure speed to shine through. 'Jody Scheckter, he was fast but he was wild,' recalled Ramirez. Everybody makes mistakes and the younger you are the more mistakes you are going to make, but at the end of the day if you're fast, it's half the battle.' Ramirez pointed out that many team principals were worried about hiring the wild ones, especially in the early days of the sport when there weren't so many sponsors and a damaged chassis might mean a team not racing that weekend, 'but it's a risk they were prepared to take. Someone like Ken Tyrrell, he was so good at talking to drivers, and made them see sense. He'd say, "OK, you're very quick, but don't try to go so quick so soon," and things like that. Ken was fantastic in that respect. I remember when Ken first had Jacky Ickx driving the car, who was one of those phenomenal people – very quick, also a bit wild. The first time he drove the car he said, "Bloody hell, so much power, Ken. I don't know if I can handle this. It's going away from me." The next day he'd say, "Ken, I think we could do with a little bit more power." That's how quick they could adjust to it.'

Sir Jackie Stewart also spoke of this maturing process. Racing drivers are good at dealing with pressure, of course, and speed and how they handle it is the greatest pressure of all. So grace under pressure is a cliché that applies in this arena. 'Jim Clark never made it look fast,' Stewart recalled. 'Keke Rosberg made it look fast, because there was a lot of sideways. And Ronnie Peterson made it look fast too, but they didn't win as much as Jim Clark. It pleased the crowd, but not the bank manager. Yet all of them had unique skills. Ronnie didn't win the world championship, but Keke did, and probably Ronnie would have done one day. Jochen Rindt had fantastic car control; you could see it all the time. Then he became very good and you didn't see it so much because he didn't need it: he had developed to a point where he didn't have to let it go to prove his skills; he could go faster without doing that. You mature into that sometimes, though some people never do.'

On the subject of speed, it wasn't long before Ramirez mentioned the name of Ayrton Senna. 'He was so unbelievably fast,' he said, 'and so many people said he was a very good test driver. I never reckoned Ayrton as a test driver, but he was so quick it didn't matter. Sometimes when he and Prost were together, he followed Prost's set-up because Prost was definitely better as a test driver than Ayrton, but Ayrton was so damn quick, and one of his biggest things was that he was able to improvise, so when the car wasn't to his liking – and 70 per cent of the time the car isn't as you'd like it to be – he could adapt himself to the car and still be quick. For Prost it was more difficult to do that.'

Ramirez added that, when Prost had the perfect car, as set up by him, he was unbeatable, but what destroyed him was Senna beating him with the very same set-up when it wasn't 100 per cent right. That's where the Brazilian's natural speed would top the Professor's engineering nous. 'Ayrton was better because he could improvise, he could keep changing – so he'd just go out and do five or six laps to get used to the car, then he'd do the quickest lap. For me, that was one of the biggest advantages that Ayrton had: he was so good at pole position, at fastest laps. Sometimes he was over a second quicker than Alain, and Alain was one of the quickest drivers there has ever been, so I don't know how he could do that, but he could. Alain was under no illusions that he could be as fast as his Brazilian team-mate. Alain was probably a bigger admirer than anybody else of Ayrton in pole position because he had the same car and he was absolutely mesmerised by how Ayrton could go so quick.'

Jackie Stewart agreed with Ramirez. He too sees Prost as the better all-round driver of the two, but not as fast. 'What a really good driver needs is an invitation, not a challenge. Prost made the car take him; Senna was taking the car. As a driver, I want to be invited to drive the car by the car, whether it's a road car or a race car. If I've got a challenge, then I'm spending more time finding the idiosyncrasies and covering for the inadequacies the car may have than I am on the creation of speed, which is my ultimate goal. So I want to eliminate those unnecessary interruptions, such as risks, hazards or distractions. If I could do that in an engineering way, through good communication with my engineers, then, instead of having performance spikes, I would have rounded experiences, so that I had more time to do things and therefore find more speed. And that's why you don't overdrive cars.'

Senna once told me about how much he hated driving the Ford-engined McLaren. Echoing Stewart, and all exceptional drivers, he complained that he was having to overdrive the car, to wrestle it around the racetrack, forcing it to do what it had to do to be competitive. He had to operate way out of his comfort area, always on the edge, and he found it nerve-racking. He knew that as a result he wasn't getting the best out of himself or the car. According to Senna, you should always drive at about 80 per cent of your maximum, so when 100 per cent is needed – for a series of fast laps in the middle of a race, for example – there is a little left over to tap into. By always having to drive on the ragged edge, Senna felt he was not driving like a champion, as he had nothing left when required to do something special. In many ways he wasn't allowing himself to be fast, to find that special space – the 'zone', as many like to call it – where he could perform at his best.

Stewart argued that speed is a function also of something more complex. 'Speed doesn't exist for a good racing driver because it's something that his or her senses are totally synchronised to,' he said. 'You don't feel speed, unless you're at 140 miles an hour, or in a bigger formula, 180 to 200 miles an hour. Everything is quite clear to you. You've got plenty of time to brake, plenty of time to shift gears, plenty of time to position the car. Only when something goes wrong, a mechanical failure or an error of judgement, does speed arise – that is, when you "react". "Oh, you must have terrific reactions," I'm often told. Well, I don't know if I could pick up a five-pound note between my fingers any faster than some kid on a street corner. What I am good at – and this is put down to reactions, which is a very simple word for a very complex combination of skills – is the consumption of information: the five-pound note's moving so I must stop it. Well, first of all you've got to see it's moving, then you've got to say, "I've got to stop it." How do I function so it goes all the way down the neuro, muscular and skeletal system for me to do that? People say it's hand–eye coordination. I say that's too simple, but it's a better definition than "reactions".'

Still Stewart wasn't happy with this definition of speed. He searched deeper. 'Right now, if somebody dropped behind my chair a 40-gallon drum that was empty, it would be a hell of a noise, and if it was a concrete floor it would be noisier. But I can bet you I wouldn't jump, because I would hear the compression of the contact and I would work it out that it wasn't dangerous. Why move if you don't have to move? Very fast sensory comprehension – not reaction, comprehension – tells you that the 40-gallon drum is not a risk to you, so why should I jump? People who are overly intense, overly nervous, sometimes overly trained, you touch them and they jump. The chances of them being very good at what they do is not so great. So, it's all about the consumption of information, the deciphering of it, the deciding on what positive action should follow from the information supplied. It shouldn't be a reactionary, undisciplined response.

'George Best could dribble and the ball never went out of control,' Stewart continued. 'He was on top of the ball's movement schedule before the ball had changed direction. Whether it was a tuft of grass or a bump, it was still accommodated for, and I'm sure Pelé was the same. Stanley Matthews in the old days, maybe Beckham today. You don't often see long movements like that in football, so some of those skills would not be relevant to today's world, and that's why someone would turn round and say, "Don't talk to me about Stanley Matthews, that's a waste of time, that's not how we do it today." But what did Stanley Matthews have inside him that allowed him to do things so much better than anybody else? Likewise George Best, and Pelé?' Or indeed a top tennis player, who seems to anticipate where a 100mph serve will bounce; or an international rugby union fly-half who reads the game as it develops around him, with 29 other players executing intricate plays and complex lines of running.

So, 'speed' and 'reaction' are misleading words. It's more a case of how quickly a person absorbs and processes information. That is what creates a cocoon of time around multiple champions. Whether they are racing drivers or top-flight achievers in other sports, all seem to have and to be able to find time, especially when all hell is breaking loose around them. In an interview Michael Schumacher gave me while testing in Barcelona before the 2003 season started, he agreed that one of the key factors in being a successful racing driver is the ability to adapt quickly to any given variable on track, to make so many vital and instant decisions in the heat of the race. 'Probably the biggest challenge you have as a racing driver, the biggest factor to affect the final result, is whether you adapt to this challenge or not,' he said. Mark Webber is on the same wavelength. 'The amount of variables make this a very frustrating sport, as so much is out of the driver's control,' he commented. 'It is hard to explain, but Tiger Woods, for example, has fewer variables to control.' This, says the Australian driver, is a constant in all branches of motor racing, from go-karts all the way up to F1. Wherever you race you have to deal with so many challenges that demand instant decisions, and all this affects the speed at which you drive. 'Lance [Armstrong] might say "It's not about the bike", but Michael could never have said "It's not about the car", because the complexity of the car is so huge that even his achievements end up being dwarfed by the variables of the electronics, set-ups, fuel mixtures and so on.'

Flavio Briatore, typically graphic in the imagery he used to describe what he looks for in a top driver, also regards raw speed as essential. 'You don't have a donkey in a horse race,' he pointed out. 'You can dress him up and groom him, but he's still a donkey.' Certainly the Italian has a stunningly good strike rate as a team manager, talent spotter and agent, a fact to which the careers of Michael Schumacher, Giancarlo Fisichella, Jarno Trulli, Mark Webber, Fernando Alonso and now Heikki Kovalainen can testify. 'A driver must know his limits,' Briatore added. 'Speed is vital, as is having the right kind of head, being cool, understanding strategy and being fit. A top driver will be consistent on the lap, lap after lap. If he drops time, it must be because the equipment is failing him, like tyres deteriorating. Top drivers are cool on the radio, they never shout, they are always calm. And they always want to know what else is happening on the track; they want to be given a sort of a freeze-frame of the race, lap after lap. With a top driver you can change strategy mid-race. The engineers won't make mistakes and if we can rely on the driver to be consistent and to change the game plan, that is a big advantage. To do this we ask them to do tough things. Like, if you want to bring them in a minute early, then they will have to do a series of very fast laps, as in qualifying, but in a race environment, lap after lap. That is the rare mark of a top driver, a fast driver.'

Briatore is, of course, not unique in looking for speed in young drivers. They all do, as it's the only way to sort through the hundreds of young drivers hoping to make it to the top. Didier Coton, the driver manager who spoke about the 'complete package' in the previous chapter, is in no doubt as to what is the most important component in the make-up of a young driver. 'You must have the speed,' he said. 'Teams, in the first place, look at the speed of drivers. The speed has to be there. If the guy doesn't have the speed, I'm not going to do it [help and train him].'

As we have already seen, Jacques Villeneuve is regarded as being more of a thinker than many of his peers in the sport. Rare in that he wore glasses and had the look of a graduate student as he sauntered about the paddock, he is clear that speed is vital, but also only a part of the mental and physical equation that allows one driver to go faster than another. 'I lived all my life with speed,' he said, 'and not only speed, but pushing the limit, pushing the envelope. Always, if there was a bridge and a bunch of snow underneath and no one else would jump it, I would make sure I jumped it and I would make sure they wouldn't. And if they jumped it, I would make sure I found a higher bridge. It's the same thing with skiing: if there's a place to go straight, you go straight, then you're happy, you've done better than the other ones, you've stretched your limit further. Same with jumping cliffs or motocross, whatever. And it's the same with a racing car. If no one used to do a section flat-out, because the car's almost on the limit, and then you did it, it didn't make you go faster, it didn't give you pole position. But the point was that you did it and nobody else did. The difference is that racing is also your job, so you think slightly differently, and if you find someone doing something better than you, you have to find a way to do it better yourself. You can always be better than you think. If you think you've got to the limit, and then someone goes faster or better, then you find a way to step up. Analyse things, and then you'll find a way to make that step up.'

Speed, pure speed, is something all drivers crave, and in their pursuit of it some lose sight of what makes a car go faster. Frank Dernie, now at Williams, has engineered some of the greatest names in F1 over a 30-year career, as well as working with Patrick Head and Ross Brawn, and is the brain behind the active suspension system. He is still baffled by the fact that, in terms of F1 racing, so many drivers don't understand what speed really is. 'I am astonished at how many people I come across who think being fast on the straights is so important while they forget that going slowly round the racetrack is not really too good,' he began with a smile. 'Let's say you do a run and you've put some new bits on the car, and you do a ten-lap sequence because you're interested in the first lap and interested in degradation at race pace. He comes in having averaged one second a lap quicker for the whole run. The driver says, "I didn't like that, I wasn't as good." "Sorry," I say, "but you are wrong. And, anyway, what's the matter?" "Well, it's a bit too pointy." "Well, OK, we'll address that. But there is no fucking way that it's worse if it was one second a lap quicker, gaining ten seconds over ten laps." There is nothing more important, and that is a fact. He might say, "I'm dead slow down the straight now", but he's faster round the racetrack. "But I won't be able to overtake anyone." I say, "You won't need to as they won't be able to catch you." The importance of being able to go fast down the straight as opposed to going faster round the lap – it's a classic. Say, for example, you come up with a set-up on the car that is worth two kilometres an hour at dot speed but is two-tenths slower around the track, the fact is you will not overtake anybody because they will be gaining on you at two-tenths a lap and disappearing into the distance.'

James Allen is another believer in the importance of speed. The ITV F1 commentator took over from British icon Murray Walker – one of the toughest asks in sports journalism – but he has made the position his own through a mixture of enthusiasm, in-depth knowledge of the workings of the paddock, and a solid and wide-ranging media track record. He was press officer at Brabham, then followed Nigel Mansell to the US where he did some TV work and wrote books before landing the ITV position ('job of a lifetime', as he describes it). Allen is uniquely positioned to observe drivers: this is, after all, what he has to do professionally on race day, live, heard by millions who see the same pictures. We are all commentators of course, and we can all see things differently. James thrives under this kind of pressure, and he is also a known face in the paddock. He knows what's going on.

He feels that F1 racers are a breed apart in so many ways, starting with speed. 'Look at all the drivers in F1,' he said. 'Come rain or shine, you go out on the circuit, on any corner of any track, anywhere in the world, and you'll say, "God, he looks quick." It's the same whether they are in a go-kart, a Formula Ford or an F1 car ... they just look quick. There's other guys who just don't. And the cream does always seem to rise to the top. You wonder about the "great lost talents", but they were lost either because they made some bad career moves or they got killed. There weren't too many that were around for a while who had the talent to really do the business and didn't get the chance to do it. This sport has become very good at not missing that talent. They might over-promote at times. We look at the pit lane and there are a few people who may not really deserve to be here. But no one gets missed. Fundamentally, the difference is speed. That is the number one thing.'

Allen then took it a little further, seeing speed as a by-product of another quality he feels it is essential for top drivers to possess. 'A heavy right foot is about nerves as much anything else. If you talk about champions, the nerves thing does come to the fore. The *Times* sports journalist Simon Barnes says that a champion is someone who combines superior skill and superior nerve. I think that is an excellent analysis because, for example, that is what makes Alonso stand out from his contemporaries.' I wondered if Allen was talking about courage, indeed fear – a touchy subject with many F1 drivers, who are unlikely to admit to any sense of fear. 'In a way, yes,' Allen agreed, 'but I mean everything: the ability to know you are in a big moment and not to choke, to deliver – whether it's a six-foot putt to win the Masters or Alonso in Brazil in 2006 – to deliver the points finish to win the championship.'

To keep your speed under the kind of pressure that is felt in F1 is not easy, and this is where grace under pressure, as Sir Jackie Stewart pointed out, does sort out the champions from the also-rans. 'Look at the single-make series like F3,' Allen continued. 'The drivers are driving for themselves, pure and simple. They will do their utmost as they are desperate to show what they can do. But when they get to F1, there is a weight that goes on to them. It's the weight of responsibility: there is a massive budget, many times bigger than the ones they were connected to in the lower formula, which they, or their backers, often had to contribute to substantially; hundreds of people, their livelihoods depending on the driver's ability to deliver the goods. To some, this is a very big burden to carry. They can be quick in a test session, but the weight gets heavier in qualifying, and then there is the race. For some it is just too much, to deliver week in and week out, through testing and race weekends.' That is when their speed goes, both in pure mph terms but also in terms of their decision-making – the areas Stewart and Schumacher pointed out as being so important.

Nerve, as Allen highlighted, is such an important component in the make-up of speed. Motor racing's rich history is littered with tales of daring, danger and death. They are constant companions for a driver throughout his career. Today's stringent safety requirements mean there are now significantly fewer fatalities (though it remains a high-risk profession), but for many years driving a racing car was truly dangerous. A mistake – or an 'off', as it is still called in a reductionist sort of way – could lead to serious injury or death. This, of course, is all part of the rich tapestry of motor racing. Danger has always added that extra something that attracts and repels at the same time; the magic and romance of the sport are deeply entwined with it. Nowadays danger is a sort of frisson, a flirtatious encounter, but when the peerless Juan Manuel Fangio was racing, and winning 24 of the 51 Grands Prix he took part in, things were different. 'In 1950 we'd reach speeds of 310kph [194mph],' the five-time world champion said in an interview, 'but of course we had front-mounted engines. And the weight distribution was so different. It was much more dangerous. The circuits were nothing like those of today. In the ten years I raced in Europe, thirty drivers were killed. Many of them were my friends.'

These days, car safety research and development as well as the nature of the racing tracks themselves, which appear to be designed with run-off areas and safety features in mind rather than racing excitement, allow modern drivers to explore the limits of the circuit and the car in a very different way from their predecessors: they just know that now they can take liberties they couldn't before. Michael Schumacher is not the only driver who has gone into the kitty litter, spun out or overshot almost every time he tested a Formula One car, but, as Sir Jackie Stewart said, 'I have never known a multiple world champion who's done that. Most of them were racing when you could not go over the limit, because the penalty was so high. Jim Clark, Graham Hill, Jackie Stewart, Niki Lauda, Nelson Piquet, Alain Prost, Ayrton Senna ... how many times did they go off the road? In my entire Formula One career, probably fewer times than the fingers on one hand, because you couldn't do it. Every now and again you'll be caught out, because the car will dig in and it will roll, and it could barrel-roll too many times for the main components to stick together, because it may stop too quickly. But now it's become OK to go off the road because the tyre walls and gravel traps have helped create a cocoon of safety that the driver sits within, together with the emergence of the very sophisticated seat – it's even retractable in the case of an accident – the HANS device, and the quality of the helmets and seatbelts. Liberties can be taken. When you race wheel to wheel at close on 200mph, in close proximity to other people, human and mechanical failures occur from time to time and these accidents can be much bigger than we've seen over these last years. The best risk management example of all in the world is Formula One. Much better than financial services, much better than road safety, much better than aero safety. Think how long ago it was since we lost a driver. And before Senna, and Ratzenberger, it was twelve and a half years.'

Once, during a long break in the middle of a cold, windy testing session at Silverstone, Ayrton Senna told me how he dealt with his fears by overcoming each incident at the time, and then building up his courage through each small victory over fear. 'As if they are bricks,' he said. And each year he had more bricks, because each year he overcame more fear. He said this calmly, and clearly he had thought it through. He added that being scared was OK; the trick was how to deal with it, and he felt that many drivers just ignored it.

It also seems to me that there are some drivers who simply lack the imagination to 'be scared' – not so much a case of being courageous, more of simply not being aware of the emotion of fear, or of denying it breathing space. Nigel Mansell was in this respect the epitome of the British army sergeant major; he would have thought nothing of charging up a heavily defended hill with just a handful of soldiers – and, of course, taking it. Damon Hill had much going on in his life, and that side of his world did front up at the races and would clearly be on his mind in some 50-50 situations. Others, like Michael Schumacher, took a clinical, reasoned approach to the issue. 'People may struggle to understand or believe this,' he said. 'This is the sport I love, and in some ways it's my job, and accidents happen every so often, and for me it's natural. Driving a car on the road is for me at times more dangerous than what I'm doing. I'm confident in what I'm doing, and the rest is fate.'

Another take on this comes from Anne Bradshaw, the doyenne of the public relations and media liaison hordes who service the teams, the drivers, the sponsors, the governing bodies, the local promoters and, of course, the press, TV and radio. Bradshaw has been in F1 since 1971 and has worked with more than thirty drivers, seven of them world champions. There is not much she does not know about drivers, and, on the subject of fear, she holds an unusual view. 'We do not talk about it with the drivers,' she stated. 'It's not on the agenda. Never has been.' Though she added that James Hunt was said to throw up before each race, she was sure the modern crop of drivers was singularly focused on the job, 'and it is a job for them, believe me. I have no doubt they look forward to Sunday. They are tense, of course, but it's tension which soon melts into exhilaration. I feel they are always in control of their environment.' In 2006, Bradshaw looked after Nick Heidfeld, Juan Pablo Montoya and newcomers Robert Kubica and Sebastian Vettel. All of them are fast drivers, and all of them, Bradshaw feels, especially the younger ones, are at ease with the various demands F1 makes of them. 'They are getting younger and younger, but they are like soldiers, in the sense that this is what they have been trained for and this is what they do best.'

Coton agrees that drivers do not seem to think too much about the dangers associated with their trade. 'I'm sure all of them think about it sometimes,' he said, 'but they put it aside. They are run by adrenalin, the excitement of racing, the unique cars and the speed they have – it's stronger than other feelings they have. Sometimes with some of them we had suspicion, but never did one of them say, "I'm going to stop because I'm too scared." They would analyse things very quickly and realise that's the way it is. No panic, nothing, just cool under pressure. They can sustain pressure very well – it's incredible the way they do that. They have a way of blocking their minds. It's a very interesting process. They may have a big off, get back in the car ten minutes later and do the time. The driver anticipates a lot; he knows exactly what's going to happen. He says, "OK, it's gone, I lost it that time." He knows how to react. If you know what will happen, you think more about protecting yourself than the feelings.' Flavio Briatore, who has seen many top drivers very close up and personal, says they do feel fear 'when they are outside the car – when they see another accident, for example. But when they put that helmet on, no, there is no fear. How could there be? So much is about self-belief, and fear has no place. Then again, to be a racing driver they have to be a bit mad, at least 15 to 20 per cent.'

Jo Ramirez agrees with Briatore that an element of madness seems to be part of the make-up. 'I just wonder where the line is,' he said. 'I think everybody has courage, but it was interesting to hear what Juan Pablo Montoya had to say one time he was trying to go past Fernando Alonso. It was a second corner, they were side by side, and both were going for it. Juan Pablo said, "I have nothing to lose. He's leading the championship. If we crash he's going to go off. I have nothing to lose, but he will have more because he wants some points, so out of the two I was 100 per cent sure he would want to slow down before me, that he would lift before me."

Obviously, he's not thinking all those things on the spur of the moment. He already knew that he had that little advantage, and it's very true. When both are leading the championship you have to be careful, but when one is leading and the other maybe hasn't got a hope, then you are on the winning side. I think they all have courage, they all have fear, but some maybe just don't demonstrate it that much. What was that race last year when somebody blew an engine and they all lifted off and Kimi [Raikkonen] didn't, and there was just a cloud of smoke but Kimi went straight through. That's fearless. Some drivers just do that. Senna used to drive in the wet when there was hardly any visibility. They just drive straight through it. I don't know what that is. Is it courage, lack of fear, madness?'

I wondered out loud if maybe it isn't just a question of not thinking of the consequences. They are racing drivers after all. They might consider having a bit of a shunt, but not a big accident. 'Possibly that has something to do with it,' said Ramirez, 'but there is another side to this.' He then made the same point Sir Jackie Stewart had made to me: 'If you think back 30 or 40 years in the sport, and you then consider how many times Michael Schumacher went off the track, you will see how driving styles have changed. Often when testing he went off the track. He also shunted very often. The point is he wanted to find the limit of the car in a particular corner or whatever, and he knew that the tracks were very safe, that the cars were very safe, and 90 per cent of the time you're not going to get hurt. How many times did Jackie Stewart or Jim Clark go off in the old days? The answer is hardly ever, because they knew if they went off they would get hurt and they didn't have another car to carry on the practice. We were all afraid to get hurt; we knew that if we went off that might be it. This is really an aspect of the sport that has changed a lot. Drivers are allowed a lot more room to find the limit of the car.'

I put it to Ramirez that perhaps engineers are pushing drivers more these days too. 'Yes, the engineers, and the whole environment,' he said. 'It's amazing how now you can work out that ten kilos of fuel is one second on a given track at a certain speed, and they don't even count the driver. You see, the driver is a machine who is going to perform exactly the same lap after lap; it's a machine that you put in the car. But he's human and he could make a mistake. Because there are less factors to make an error, everything is so predictable. The engineers, like Neil Martin at McLaren, they do every calculation and that's it. They don't consider that the driver might sneeze as that's not part of the deal.'

Finally, on the subject of the strange cocktail that makes up speed, Ramirez remarked upon the ability some drivers have to be immediately quick. In the car, and off. 'Stewart was one of those guys who was extremely cool, and he was always very quick from the beginning. Senna was the same: he approached the first corner like he was flying, really on it already. It's not the same for all drivers. For some, as their breathing is very fast at the start, it takes them a lap or two to get their normal breathing pattern back and into race mode. By then the Stewarts, Sennas and Schumachers are long gone. All the top guys are very much like that.'

These people born with natural speed – the big right foot – are now being groomed from the earliest age to perform on the highest stage of all. This means all is taken care of for them so that they can focus on one thing only: how to go faster. For these top young drivers, long gone are the days, recent as they were, recalled by Webber: 'When I used to race in F3 I used to turn up in a 1.1 Ford Fiesta; others turned up in BMW M3s and had never worked a day in their lives. It made me stronger.' There is, however, one other big variable to be taken into account, and we have already touched on the issue. Something that can make the big right foot press hard on the pedal or maybe lift a little in the 'wrong' places. That is the head, or the brain, or the mind – the part of the body that can make or break a driver's career.

CHAPTER THREE

A BEAUTIFUL MIND

Testing at Silverstone. It's cold and damp and a young Mika Hakkinen, not yet a champion driver, is putting a McLaren through its paces. The car is being pushed back into the garage, rear-end first. Mika is still strapped in. Walking alongside the car, clipboard in hand, earphones on and a frown on his face, is race engineer Giorgio Ascanelli. Impatient, fiery, brilliant – not the man you would normally associate with the grey-cool world of Ron Dennis – the Italian is trying to get Mika to tell him about the car. Something has gone wrong, but Mika seems unable to speak the same language as Ascanelli. English is, of course, the common form of communication in most F1 teams, but Giorgio's fast, chewed-up diction and the Finn's slow, deliberate delivery are not to blame for the engineer's frustration. Ascanelli starts waving his arms about – he's getting angry. Finally, he walks away, tearing his earphones off. 'All he can say is there is a failure,' he complains. 'Yes, I know – a brain failure!' The pit crew are a little surprised. Maybe this kind of outburst goes on in some of the smaller teams, but at McLaren? Drivers at this level are clear, cogent and concise in their feedback. But Mika is still young and very shy, and he clearly found dealing with the overpowering Ascanelli just too much. He is, after all, a senior engineer at McLaren, used to dealing with Ayrton Senna, at that time the best driver in the world.

A big right foot, essential though it is, is not enough. A driver needs to communicate extensively with the team in the pits, especially the race engineer. And of course a race engineer needs to communicate with the driver. Stefano Sordo is Scott Speed's race engineer at Scuderia Toro Rosso. Viewed against the might of McLaren, or Ferrari, this is indeed a small team with an inexperienced driver. So, do they have a chat about football and girls, maybe kick the tyres, and then out he goes? Not quite. Even at this level – and I don't mean any disrespect as I know how much hard graft goes into working in a less-funded team – the relationship and its complexity are apparent. In a piece he wrote for the *Red Bulletin*, the satirical F1 magazine printed at all the races, Sordo summed up beautifully the relationship between Speed and himself at the sharp end of testing, racing and decision-making. (Sordo, by the way, is a wonderful surname for a race engineer as it means 'deaf' in Italian – most definitely an occupational hazard in the pits. Speed is, of course, another great name.)

The media likes to say that the relationship between a driver and his race engineer is crucial to the success of the team. So, what do we actually do? Well, race engineering isn't just about the mechanical set-up of the car. It's also about tuning the car to the driver's liking. It's important to know what he wants, what he needs, and the difference between the two.

This is my favourite example. In simulation the difference between the best and worst set-up might only be three- or four-tenths; if you apply those criteria in the real world, the difference might be a couple of seconds. The driver has limits that the pure mathematics don't consider. In a very real sense, the driver amplifies the set-up.

And so it's important to understand how the driver feels and to know what the driver likes. In a mechanical environment it's a human relationship, and if you are close to the driver, the better that relationship is. It isn't just a question of set-up, it's the complete strategy for the weekend, dealing with issues like does your guy feel confident running all day Friday on just one set of tyres, or will you get more out of using two?

Overall it's a confident driver that makes the car go faster. You will have days where the car is set up a tenth slower than the absolute theoretical optimum, but the driver can drive it quicker. Some drivers are comfortable with a very low level of downforce, others are not. Sometimes you will want to give away a little bit of top speed to make the driver confident. It's a balancing act. You can find yourself in a situation where the car might be easy to drive, but isn't quick enough, or have a car that in theory is very quick, but the driver just isn't happy with it. Ultimately the car only goes as fast as he can drive it. You have to find the best compromise. The team is in the sweet spot when the theoretical model and the set-up the driver enjoys are as close as possible. The race engineer has a pretty easy weekend when that happens.

Time builds your rapport. You learn to calibrate a driver's feelings as you get used to listening to his feedback. We're now at race sixteen [in 2006], so I've been working with Scott for the past fifteen races. I'm lucky because he's precise in his feedback, but regardless, you become accustomed to hearing what the driver is saying. In the first few races it can be difficult, especially if the driver is new to F1, but it is vital that you learn to understand one another quickly. A team can't afford to have the driver and his race engineer spending ten minutes between runs trying to figure out the sense of what the other is trying to say. If you understand quickly, you can make changes quickly, and that can have a huge influence on the weekend. Of course when you're working quickly, both sides have to take the other on trust. From a race engineer's point of view, if the driver doesn't trust you, and understand what you're doing and why you're doing it, then frankly, it's a waste of time.

And it is not just a question of trust among professionals. There is much more to it than that, and much of it has to do with the idiosyncrasies of the driver. And drivers are quite a complicated bunch of individuals. Frank Dernie, the veteran race engineer now at Williams, is clear that all drivers, at least the best ones, share one character trait. 'Drivers are introverts,' he observed. 'All the great drivers, especially the multiple champions, are introverts. The ability to concentrate is a characteristic of introverts. On the other hand, extroverts are affected by what I think in psychology are called "involuntary rest poses", periods during which they are not really concentrating at all. They are completely unaware of this; they think they are, but they are not. And in a racing car you could have gone a very long way in that time. Also, statistics show that extroverts have many more accidents than introverts. A lot of bus and taxi companies now give personality tests to applicants and won't hire the extroverts because of their accident record. You have an accident in a racing car and you ain't going to be winning the race, are you?'

So we have introverted drivers who need to communicate their feedback to usually very experienced technical staff. No wonder Mika Hakkinen struggled in the early days. Dernie understands the problem, and pointed out that it's really not easy for the drivers to adapt initially. 'The mental side is key really. These drivers are fast, but they also have to deal with the engineers. The engineer needs to have a good relationship with the drivers because, with all due respect to all the drivers I have dealt with and spoken to, the likelihood of them understanding the engineering, especially in the early stages of their career, is zero.' He added that race engineers are incredibly capable individuals who have been to university and studied vehicle dynamics and aerodynamics at the highest possible level, 'and who still take years to understand how the car works. Therefore a 21-year-old-driver who's had five years on the job is no match for them.' They might have the capacity to create an instinctive link between what they see and what is occurring, which may or may not be right, 'but one of the most difficult things as an engineer is when you have a driver who is absolutely convinced in his own mind that what he is feeling is such and such when you know it can't be, and you have great difficulty in explaining this to him without leaving him feeling very insulted that you don't believe him.'

This pig-headedness, so common in drivers, who have perforce to be egocentric, selfish and sure of themselves, can indeed lead to difficulties in the relationship, especially when the engineer has to gather data and at the same time convince the driver that he, the driver, is wrong about something, and the available data point to the engineer being right. 'You are not going to question their driving line,' Dernie said, 'or you shouldn't, unless you can see something like the track is rubbered-in where they can't see it. You might tell them to try a tighter line here – they would be able to see that way before you would, that is their thing – but, generally speaking, if a driver comes in, you might get things like, "The chassis is flexing. I can feel it flexing." Well of course they bloody can't. Absolutely no possibility whatsoever that the driver can feel the chassis flexing. So now you have a situation where you have a person who is absolutely convinced the chassis is flexing, and he can't possibly be right. So what do you say? Do you say, "We'll stick it in the rig and check it." Or do you say, "Don't talk such complete bollocks, it must be something else." It is a difficult one. Luckily it's not often the great drivers who talk bollocks. But I've had drivers telling me, "My chassis is flexing, and it's worse in the wet." Well, that can't be true, as if the chassis is flexing one thing that will fix it is running in the wet, when the loads are down. But two and two did not make four in the mind of this particular driver, who shall remain nameless. It really is one of the most difficult problems for an engineer to deal with: how to put the driver right without him taking offence. It depends on the driver, as some don't expect to understand, but, still, the most important relationship is one of mutual trust between driver and engineer.'

So, like Sordo, and all other engineers, Dernie emphasised this issue of trust, earned in the most pressurised of circumstances. 'I'm lucky,' he continued, 'I'm in F1. There are no slow drivers in F1. Some fans may say so-and-so is "a wanker", but, believe me, none of them are. Even the least fast one is still spectacularly fast and brilliant by any normal standards. And this is the man, often a young man, you need to develop a rapport with by which you are able to ask him where you are losing lap time. That is what you need to know. You don't need an essay, you don't need fifty pages on how the car handles in each phase of a corner, you just need to focus on which corner the shortcomings of the car cause the most detriment to lap time. That is the key issue. If you are doing that – and as an engineer you understand the car well enough to take what he is saying and say "A-ha! What we need to improve is this and this" – then between the two of you you can explain what is happening in the right place.'

Dernie has, of course, seen many drivers come and go. But what does it feel like from the other side? Robert Doornbos is typical of the new breed of drivers: multilingual, affable, excellent with the media, bright and engaging, with a fair amount of money behind him, if it were needed. He's an excellent all-round sportsman whose skills range from kickboxing to tennis, both of which he practised at the highest level in certain age groups. He is also in the middle of a business degree. He raced for Minardi in 2005, and in 2006 continued his learning by driving for Red Bull Racing as the team's third and test driver. His impressions of his first outings in an F1 car, as told to the *Red Bulletin* during the European GP in Germany, are quite revealing.

I had the perfect grounding in F3000 [which he won in 2004] before coming to F1. You get to learn ten major European circuits and you have to adapt to getting on the pace quickly as there is no testing and the tyres would go after one lap. It was hard, but by the time I came to F1 I had all the skills necessary. In F1, the pressure to get things right is immense. You have to be able to drive on the limit straight away to get the maximum from the tyres, to give the right feedback. You have to push very hard, and that's difficult. But to be honest I enjoy that challenge. It's great fun finding that limit quickly.

I was amazed at the technology that was available when I came into F1. It's a whole other skill set. To be able to adjust everything all the way round is amazing. To get used to adjusting the traction control and the diff settings when I was going into and out of corners, and doing that every time, was hard. Before I came in I don't think I could even play on a PlayStation, but now I'm like a programmer.

Quite a jump up then, with a lot of room to get it wrong – and this is a guy with a clear, cogent, concise mind who could be top of any class he cared to join.

This is why Giorgio Ascanelli was having a tantrum at that Silverstone test: he was not getting the correct feedback. He certainly received it from Ayrton Senna. When I worked at McLaren I was allowed to wear the team headphones. Of course I had nothing to contribute to the engineering and tactical process, but it was fascinating to listen to the exchanges between the team members. Most interesting of all was when a driver was pushed back into the pits after a testing session or a qualifying run. The most impressive, freakishly so, was Senna. As he stopped the car outside the pits and the mechanics walked towards him to push him back into the garage, the Brazilian would say, 'Steve?' Steve Hallam, Senna's race engineer, would reply, very calmly as usual, 'Yes, Ayrton?' And then Senna would go into an extraordinary world of his own, quite literally downloading information from the nose cone of the car to the rear wing. Nothing was missed; all was analysed, dissected, evaluated and delivered to Hallam and his team of engineers, fuel experts and all the other people who had a contribution to make. The words, robotic nearly, were seamless, just one long sentence, never faltering, never stopping for thought. It had all been absorbed, worked out and stored in the man's racing brain.

But of course not all great drivers are, or were, like Senna. 'I remember one great driver who was concerned he was losing time at Copse at Silverstone,' recalled Dernie. 'We weren't slow, but we were not making much of an improvement, working quite hard on the car, and when the session ended we were fastest at Copse, by quite some margin, so he had misjudged the shortcoming of the car and we'd spent the whole hour of the practice working on the car for a section of the circuit where he was already fastest. To give another example, Alan Jones [world champion in 1980] really did not care how the car worked but was very good at highlighting understeer at the hairpin. You knew that was what was slowing the car down, but he didn't really care what you did about it. If you told him, "I think I'll stick softer front springs on", he might say something like, "Yes, but the car is already a little unstable in the fast corner. Is there anything else?" But he would not have mentioned the instability at all had you not suggested that adjustment. If the adjustment you were going to make was softer rear anti-roll bar, he might well have never mentioned it until it became the most pressing problem. So you need to do the right thing first, the most important. Getting the sequence and zeroing in rapidly is the most important thing, and not all drivers do that very well. Not all engineers can read their driver either.'

Now that the sport has relaxed its rules a little with regard to pit-to-car radio transmissions, we can now occasionally eavesdrop on some of the interchanges between engineer and driver. Well, not interchanges, more like one-way traffic as the man back at base is telling the driver what to do. And despite all the complicated technology on the car, the myriad buttons on the steering wheel and the constant adjusting a driver is required to do – be it brake balance, fuel mixture or any number of other operations aimed at maximising a car's performance during the changing conditions of a Grand Prix – you still most often hear the engineer's voice urging his driver to overtake, to close a gap, to post three fast laps at such and such a time, basics that could be shouted by any keen dad at any local karting event. And that is the sort of relationship that often develops between driver and engineer: that of a mentor instructing his younger charge on how to behave in a rarefied, unforgiving environment.

In this respect, Dernie has an anecdote to tell concerning a young Michael Schumacher. 'When I first joined Benetton in 1992, Michael would not go testing. He was a Grand Prix driver now and he felt the test driver could do the testing. If you did want him to go to a test, he would arrive having flown from Germany, then complain about the traffic, having arrived at 10.30 at Silverstone – too late to do the debrief – and by three in the afternoon he'd be saying "Have we finished yet?" and wanting to get the next plane home. To go from there, to make him realise that it was the testing that was going to make him go quicker, was not easy. It took a long time. I was spectacularly exasperated with him. We'd go to a race meeting where I was race-engineering him and he would not want to fit any of the bits we had found to work in the testing because he had not tested them. It used to drive me mad. Ross [Brawn] was more patient with him. The man you see now, this great driver, did not come naturally, believe me. The importance of testing had to be beaten into him over a long period. Now he is a seven-time world champion.'

Another multiple world champion who is a very interesting person to talk to about what makes a driver tick, or not, at the highest level – because he has had to do most things in his profession the hard way – is Andy Priaulx, who, since 2004, has won the World Touring Car Championship with BMW three times in a row (a fact generally accepted in motor racing circles, even though in 2004 it was actually called the European Touring Car Championship; some of the circuits were, in fact, outside Europe, and the format and cars etc. were the same). The affable yet highly competitive Guernseyman is not a regular F1 driver, though he has tested a number of times. In his case a lack of sponsorship in his early years of racing counted against him, but he still rose to the top of his game and, as he is fond of saying, tongue in cheek, he is the only British motor racing world champion.

'Driving a car is all about feeling,' he said. 'You've got the data to give you an idea where you're losing it, but you've got to translate that data to a feeling, and that's what's difficult. What's it going to feel like in the car? The data engineer can say you're losing time, that your minimum speed is low, but they can't say it's going to feel a bit like this, this is how you overcome it, by looking a little further ahead . . . they can't tell you that. And a lot of natural drivers, the most gifted ones, when they reach that barrier they don't know how to overcome these issues. That's when a guy who's worked at it does know and can overcome it. I've heard Gerhard Berger say that very often the working driver can get to a higher level than the natural driver because he works at it, he understands it.'

Dernie and Priaulx agree to differ on this, as do most driver/engineer combinations. But that is only right as their jobs are so different and their points of focus so diverse, though the end result must be the same. Then again, there are other ways of focusing on the job at hand. Dernie recalled another driver who seemed to be very single-minded about what he wanted. Trouble was, this was not at all what the engineers were after. 'He was not interested in the gear ratios until he had pulled the best girl in the paddock and grabbed the best hotel room. Basically, the first day of practice was a washout as his entire focus was on his needs. He would not even turn up at debriefs. Until all that was sorted you did not have his attention. That is extreme, though ...'

Extreme, but all too common before the really big money came into the sport and a different work ethic prevailed. Now drivers are highly disciplined, like any other professional sportsmen, and the challenges for them are rather different. They will be coming from a smaller team where they will have a driven a car that will have been bought in, and where the engineer's input will not have been anywhere near the level it's at in F1. 'He will find himself in a massive organisation,' Dernie confirmed, 'being pushed from pillar to post. It's much, much more difficult to cope with the PR demands which are thrust in your face than the engineering ones. It is true that it is a big change technically to have a race engineer thrust on you who knows the car backwards, usually because they conceived it. All the other racing they have done they have generally bought something and the bloke who runs it knows a bit about it, or nothing at all. It is a massive step, but it's probably a bigger thing to cope with bag carriers, trainers, television, sponsors' requirements and so on, which take up so much of their time.'

Bag carriers. A commonly used expression for the motley crew that surrounds so many of the drivers. Some are quite literally just that – helmet and bag carriers. Strange but true: these people really exist, and usually in the smaller teams. Michael Schumacher had no bag carrier. He had a personal press officer, and in some countries he did avail himself of discreet security, but that was the extent of his 'crew'. For others it is different. 'Many drivers are shy,' pointed out Anne Bradshaw, the much-travelled and wonderfully helpful media liaison for BMW. 'They have a very sheltered existence and find it hard to cope with all the people in the paddock, even in their own motor home. So they bring their support with them.' This squares with Frank Dernie's view of drivers being introverts, ill at ease in social environments they cannot control. But there are exceptions of course. Juan Pablo Montoya, a big loss to F1 and surely a great find for Nascar, was popular with his mechanics and, though prone to moods, he was always ready to have a laugh with them. He'd often turn up in the garage at ten in the morning, a full hour before start of practice, to talk, observe, and generally be part of the team. But someone like Ralf Schumacher enters the pits at 10.59, putting his helmet on. The less exchange, the better.

Bradshaw told me that a great many drivers worry about their equipment, from the engine to the helmet, and generally feel insecure, so many devise strategies to develop their own world around them, so as to feel protected. This reminded me of speaking with Nigel Mansell in 1991, after he left Ferrari and rejoined Williams. The interview took place at his Ferrari dealership in the West Country, and he told me how leaving the Italian team had been a wrench but that he welcomed the chance of driving for an English team. 'I feel I'm back in my comfort zone,' he said. That's an important place to be for many F1 drivers. Despite the rich-boy trappings, the helicopters and the fat wristwatches, not to mention the large property portfolios and the even larger bank accounts, there is an all-pervading sense of insecurity sweeping around the world of F1.

James Allen, always an astute paddock watcher, summed it up very well when he remarked that a lot of it has to do with desperation. A strong word to use in the context of multi-millionaires, but Allen stuck to his guns. 'I think this is an important part of the driver's make-up,' he said. 'How secure do they feel? Can you imagine in your job, if you were not really sure now if you had an income next year. And for a driver this could be the case on an annual basis. This is a very stressful thing to deal with, cushioned slightly by the fact that by now you have made a couple of quid or maybe your dad has loads of money and you won't have to sell matches at Piccadilly Circus. Nevertheless, there are a lot of people in this position. You need a great degree of self-reliance to cope with this and not let this turn to desperation, and for this desperation not to appear in your driving. You need self-belief and the knowledge that you can do it.

'Martin Brundle was very high on skills,' Allen added, mentioning the man who works as the analyser alongside him in the ITV booth. 'But looking back on his career he feels he lacked the total self-confidence that Senna had. And we mustn't forget Brundle was fighting Senna for the F3 championship. He was nearly too considerate, and there were a very few times in his career when he was a total and utter twat to the people around him, and therefore utterly ruthless and massively successful. But it wasn't really in his nature.' Hence Brundle's relative underachievement, when many, like Allen, felt he had the skill to get to the very top.

There is no doubt the great champions possess an element of arrogance, coldness, aloofness, selfishness … all words that describe only parts of their complex make-ups. Senna was famously seen as being arrogant; even his religious faith was mocked by fellow drivers and some of the media. He was correct to a fault, sometimes creating waves around him through his desire to do the right thing. Once, when I was working for McLaren as their press officer, I approached him after a qualifying session for the usual quote that would help to fill up the bland press release all teams give out after each session. The less adventurous journalists, those who never seem to leave the media centre, devour these sheets of information, but no one else takes them too seriously as they hide more than they reveal. Senna, upset by an underperforming Ford engine, refused to give me a statement. When I pushed him, he lost his temper. 'What do you want to me to say?' he shouted. 'It's shit. It's a shit engine, and that is all I can say. Why should I lie? And you, Norman, as someone I respected when you were a journalist, you shouldn't be asking me to lie.' He was right, of course, and he hit me where it hurt, especially as I had huge dollops of respect and admiration for this extraordinary and self-contained man.

For a while his race engineer, Giorgio Ascanelli, gave me the quotes I needed, and Senna and I hardly spoke. Which was a tough call for me as I was in charge of media relations for a very high-profile team. Then one day Senna's own press officer came to me with one of the blue baseball caps Senna wore for his Brazilian banking sponsor Nacional. 'Ayrton heard you had a son and he thought he might like this,' she said, and gave me the cap. 'Best wishes, Ayrton' was autographed on the fabric. My son still has the cap, and I have the memory of a man who could play hardball and mind games with anyone, but who was also very humble and considerate to those around him.

When I put it to Bradshaw that drivers are inherently selfish, she disagreed. 'Self-centred, yes. Selfish, no. And I make that distinction because racing drivers are always part of a team, while a tennis player, or a golfer, are more individual sportsmen and they can become selfish. But not racing drivers, when they have to interact with so many people who make it possible for them to drive the car out of the garage.' She added that a good driver will get the best out of a team, and in turn teams will do absolutely anything for their driver. Mark Webber agreed with this. 'It's important to keep a team at arm's length and yet create a situation where they will walk over hot coals for you. The key is to be extremely professional and do your best, always. I got into this game very late and I'm happy to spend time with the guys after the race. But there has to be rhythm and consistency about my work, which is about being professional.'

It is a complicated relationship, as outlined by Dernie earlier in this chapter. The waters are muddied further by the bag carriers, of course, and also by the presence of parents and family. 'There are more fathers about and fewer wives,' Bradshaw observed. This seems not to work so well as in the past. Wives, and girlfriends, were welcome because they generally helped with the running of the team. There are lovely, evocative black and white photographs of Nina Rindt, wife of Jochen, on the pit wall looking stunning and clutching a stopwatch and a clipboard. That was in the 1960s, but until quite recently wives and girlfriends had a strong presence in the paddock, which was all the better for it. A nice mixture of normality and glamour. 'A little while ago, the wives quite literally helped look after their husbands,' Bradshaw continued. 'The teams had a friendlier feel and everyone talked to each other around the paddock. Now, everything is done for the driver, and it is more like going to work every day. And as the drivers get younger, and the potential earnings soar, it is fathers who have made their presence felt.'

Bradshaw, who also works in the BMW junior series, said she gets her fill of crying, hysterical parents and does not understand why drivers are not left to their own devices once they hit the big stage. 'After all, if your son was an accountant, you wouldn't follow him to his office every day, sit down beside him and grab free cups of coffee, would you?' Of course, as one myself, I know that fathers want their sons to do well, and in the case of sport we do run the risk of burdening them with our own expectations, frustrations and so on. As a result, a young driver who comes in with a strong mental side is immediately respected by his peers, whatever his age. 'I saw Nelson [Piquet] Jr crying in Monaco,' Bradshaw said, 'and I look at Nico Rosberg. The two boys have had such a different upbringing from Keke and Nelson. I know which one will do better. Now everyone knows Nelson Jr is vulnerable. When a driver loses his cool, the team should be there to protect him. But it's important not to show any emotions. We are all different, but you have to project aura from start to finish. It's a constant message, and it's so much about mind games.'

Mark Webber is a graceful, lean man with a degree of delicacy about him, like a finely tuned cheetah. Yet he is famously super-fit and immensely tough mentally, and is not averse to resorting to the hardman Aussie stereotype to get his point across. 'You do what is right for you,' he said. 'The mentality in my house when I grew up was to "have a go". It's the Aussie way: never give up, because giving up is the easy option.' Of course Webber is no fool and he can see beyond the tough Aussie façade: 'But never giving up can also be the wrong option. Survival in the rain, for example – you have to draw the line somewhere. But still, pushing myself to the limit – that is what I get out of bed for every day, and I relish the tougher days as you feel more complete when you have got through them. You cannot get away from the truth that this is personal, that you have to train hard as you are in a very tough environment with very tough individuals.'

Mental hardness comes from genes, environment, desire and adversity. Webber had the kind of upbringing that seems nearly old-fashioned amid all the modern-day debates on child obesity and computer games. 'I grew up outdoors and loved and played all sports, particularly rugby league,' he reminisced. 'I was from a small town and we developed the small-town, small-team mentality. It was always a struggle and a fight against the odds. The others were from bigger towns and bigger teams so we always went out with a nothing-to-lose mentality and the underdog hardness that comes with it. I loved the one-on-one of league, the tackling especially. I even went through a stage of wanting to hurt people in the tackle, to get them on their back foot. My dad played rugby union. He was a very competitive individual. He had a motorbike shop but he would not let me race motorbikes.'

Webber raced cars instead, but his talent lulled him into taking it easy. By his own admission he was 'pretty laid back'. 'The competitive edge really came through when I came to Europe,' he explained. 'That's when I began to grasp what Steve Waugh and Mick Doohan were all about. It's about upsetting people, getting an edge; the right mind attitude is essential. When I raced in Europe for Mercedes in 1998/99, I thought to myself, "I am a pro now", and I felt very good about myself. But it was no joke at first. There I was, twenty years old, racing grown men who knew all the tricks, and who made sure they used them on me. I learnt very quickly to turn bad experiences into positives. Bottom line is you have their respect if they are trying to mess you up. You learn to pick up on the body language. Then I enjoyed racing. Now it's about testing myself.'

The hardening process, first started on the baked rugby

fields of Queanbeyan, really kicked in at Le Mans in 1999 when Webber survived a horrendous 185mph crash. 'In many ways I was a late developer, and when I flipped over in Le Mans and very nearly lost my life, that really put fire in my belly. I was out for five months, house bound. I got myself fit and ready but I was off the radar; there was no telephone ringing. At the time Thierry Boutsen said I would never race again. That was a comment that had a real effect on me, as he was an F1 driver and his opinion mattered. Within two hours of the accident I promised myself I would not go back to sports cars. With Anne [Neal, his partner], I decided I would only drive single-seaters. In those months I became very, very determined to make it and promised myself that nothing would stop me.'

So, F1 drivers not only need an ability to interact and understand engineers, they need to be resilient and focused, and of course they need to be mentally tough. All this can easily spill into areas that become unpleasant. 'There is a fine line between showing happiness after a win and disrespect,' Webber pointed out. 'It is the line between emotion and arrogance.' But, for James Allen, 'arrogant is a word that would only be used by a third party to describe you. You would never use this word to describe yourself. Maybe self-reliant, confident, and so on, but not arrogant. Ultimately, history is written by the winners. The ultimate judgement will be purely based on their success, not on whether they were arrogant.' Just like Ayrton Senna, Michael Schumacher was often described as arrogant by the media, and his successor Fernando Alonso is usually referred to as 'cold' – surely just a short step away from being dubbed 'arrogant'.

This may make it harder to interview them, but it sure as hell helps them focus on the huge job they have to do as the spearhead of a big, demanding team. There is no room for error. A healthy dose of self-confidence, indeed arrogance, is clearly part of the job description.

The beautiful mind is also required to keep things under control, of course, especially when the heart is pounding at the start of a race. Being on the grid in the minutes leading up to the moment when the lights go off is one of the most memorable things you can do in motor racing. The tension is palpable as the drivers focus on the race to the first corner, going over the tactics, wondering what the car on the right will do, or the one behind, where the best, stickiest bits of tarmac are, and so on. This is when their hearts race up to 200 beats per minute, pounding away in the head and chest. And all the while their hearts are trying to burst out of their chests, they are tightly strapped in, immobile.

Drivers use a variety of techniques to cope with this unusual situation. Indeed, the preparation can start some way away from the starting grid, as Robert Doornbos explained. 'On Thursdays it's really good to walk the track and get to know what it's like,' he said. 'We come once a year and we have to re-think it all the time. These days it's great because we have bikes. They give you the idea of what the bumps and hollows are like. There are physical and mental aspects you have to get right. Personally I take time to get my heart rate up and my mind focused before getting in the car, so when I go out I'm at the right pace immediately. I have the right rhythm before even starting.'

In Buenos Aires in 1992 I had the honour of interviewing Juan Manuel Fangio, for many people still the best driver there has ever been. He had a simple approach to getting his head in the right place at the right time. 'So much has to do with preparation,' he stated. 'If the car goes well, the driver is just another element. But when the car is a bad one, that is when the really good drivers, the strong ones, come to the fore. Just like in life, motor racing favours those with character, like Tazio Nuvolari, or Jim Clark, who was one of the best drivers ever. And Niki Lauda, Jackie Stewart, then Alain Prost, and Ayrton Senna. This year the hardest-working team has been Williams, and the results are for all to see.' Fangio was a great admirer of the British team. 'They have done miracles. Frank Williams has chosen his staff very well, and now you can see the results. A good team is so important. It gives the driver time and confidence to express himself. When I raced with the Mercedes team I had a huge advantage: the cars would not break down.' Senna at McLaren-Honda, Mansell at Williams, Schumacher at Ferrari, Alonso at Renault – along with Fangio, they all had that one vital factor in common: a fast car that didn't break down. Nothing better to ease any jitters or uncertainties in the driver's mind.

To iron out his uncertainties, Andy Priaulx resorted to meditation. He had a tough time establishing himself in the upper echelons of motor racing. Lack of funds and a subsequent and linked spell of 'driver's block' caused him to re-examine and reinvent himself to an extent. 'I got to the stage where I almost became desperate for performance,' he explained. 'I was prepared to do anything to win a race, just to prove I could win. I started to apply myself and look around, and I had a friend who'd done meditation and he recommended it to me because my biggest problems were off-track, not on-track: I couldn't get the funding, I couldn't get the right team; then I couldn't get the right team, so I couldn't get the right result; and so on. So I started to do meditation and visualising the various problems I had, finding various solutions which I'd never have thought about had I not visualised them, using various techniques to key into the young driver I once was, one who just got into any car he was given and drove well. I tried to find those feelings of natural driving again, taking away the pressure of money and everything else, driving like I loved to drive. Meditation taught me how to trap that natural intuitive driving, how to overcome the big problems of money and try to focus on ideal solutions. I still use it now, and I've won back-to-back titles in one of the toughest championships outside Formula One.'

It's not all about individualistic solutions, of course. Like Webber, Priaulx is a strong believer in teamwork. Both drivers subscribe to the work ethic that you are only as good as your weakest link. A lot of drivers purely rely on natural ability, which can only get you so far in motor racing. 'You've got to get the team around you,' Priaulx insisted. 'You've got to attract the team. Like Senna. He had something infectious about him; he attracted the team. He praised his team with scant praise; they didn't need much praise to feel that they'd really achieved something. I've been working a little bit with Mansell and you can see how he'd manipulate things his way. Schumacher's the same, and I'm sure Alonso's the same. You've got to attract people. Very often my teams at the beginning of the season hated me, and by the end of the season they loved me. That's how it should be really. The only way to truly reward a team is with results. A team wants the performance, but they want to see that you've worked for that performance. It's difficult to win on your good day, it's extremely difficult to win on your bad day. What makes a true champion or true sportsman is a guy who can perform when things aren't quite right around him. He can turn things around when his back's against the wall and get the result he needs.'

The last words on the subject of how the head must rule the body have to be Sir Jackie Stewart's. In 1968 he won a legendary race at the Nürburgring – the full fourteen-mile circuit, of course – in torrential rain. I and many others have marvelled at this feat, impossible even to consider for us lesser mortals, just in terms of the level of concentration needed to drive round somewhere like that. 'That's where the mind management has to work at the highest level,' Stewart said, 'because your knowledge of where the circuit's going has to be so profound that you commit to the speeds and high gears over blind areas where the car's light coming down and where you know you can do things. That intimacy with the circuit is really paramount. There are some great escape artists, people who can do amazing recoveries, but the recovery uses up a lot of track, time and distance. There are some places at the Nürburgring where that drops you back a very long way. And you can't keep doing that at the

Nürburgring or you'll eventually make a mistake: it'll take you off the road where there's no space to go off the road.

'The Nürburgring was the biggest challenge simply because it was 187kph [117mph] when I first went there in 1965, and it went like that till 1968. Then it was changed, and we got it easier – much wider, a better surface. But even then it was quick. There were fewer corners so it came down to 170-odd, I think. But to know that and to be able to go for it and be able to repeat it you had to be below the threshold of your absolute ability, and I never did a lap of the Nürburgring that I didn't want to do. Everybody said they loved the Nürburgring. Bullshit. They were either telling lies or they weren't quick enough around it.'

CHAPTER FOUR

PAY DRIVER

In the winter of 1990, Jordan driver Bertrand Gachot, the French son of a European Commission official, got into a fight with a London taxi driver and sprayed the man with CS gas. Fast forward to August 1991, and a judge sentences Gachot to six months in Brixton prison, one of England's worst. This altercation and the draconian sentence started a chain of events that led to Michael Schumacher winning seven world titles and Gachot fading from the Formula One scene after a couple of abortive comebacks.

That all this happened at Jordan was no surprise, for Eddie Jordan had made the handling of pay drivers into an art form. An Irishman of some business acumen, he was already wealthy through running his F3 and F3000 teams when he joined the Formula One circus, where he unearthed some great drivers and smilingly fleeced a great many more. He brought back to F1 a degree of levity and piratical derring-do which made for good copy for him and his team (maybe less so for some of his sponsors) and kept him busy for years going in and out of the motor home and London office of the Great Buccaneer himself, Bernard Charles Ecclestone, who in the end snatched the biggest prize of all from Jordan's grasp.

When Gachot was sentenced and locked up, Eddie
Jordan, or 'EJ' as he was known, needed a driver for the
Belgian GP at Spa-Francorchamps, one of the greatest
circuits on the F1 calendar and the most demanding of a
driver's skill and courage. It has been suggested that EJ was
not hugely displeased that Gachot would not be driving
since he had already taken the Frenchman's money for the
season and therefore saw the opportunity of cashing in on
some more much-needed funds. He was in fact prepared to
pay to put in an experienced driver like Keke Rosberg or
Derek Warwick who would be able to do a good job in an
unfamiliar car around such a demanding circuit. But then
he was contacted by people acting on behalf of a young
German driver by the name of Michael Schumacher.

The story is taken up by Ian Phillips, who at the time
was the commercial and marketing director at Jordan
Grand Prix and is now at Spyker F1, the team that arose out
of the ashes of Midland F1, which before that was called
Jordan Grand Prix. Phillips, a former editor of *Autosport*
who helped start up and run the March and Leyton House
F1 teams, is a gregarious and very well-informed motor
racing insider who has lived through most of the
permutations the sport can throw up. Phillips had been
working on getting a regular, experienced driver for Jordan
for the Belgian race, but 'suddenly I got a call on the Sunday
night the week before the race from Eddie saying there is a
guy called Michael Schumacher coming tomorrow
morning, give him a seat fitting and give him a test. He will
be driving; Mercedes are paying £150,000 for this race and

possibly thereafter. He turned up on Monday and did the seat fitting. Then Tuesday we did a test on Silverstone's south circuit. After four laps Trevor Foster, our team manager, said, "I'm going to call him in: he's going too fast. This guy's frightening us with what he is doing with the car. Go and find Eddie and tell him we've found a star." That was it basically.' Phillips insisted that despite their reputation for uncovering great talent, Schumacher was not really on the Jordan radar. EJ might have seen him race at Macau in F3, but other than that he was unknown in the paddock, though there were a few whispers about him. The point is, he was taken on as a pay driver.

There was, of course, a plan behind it all. Gachot and his CS gas canister opened the way for a major involvement from German motor manufacturers in F1. Schumacher, together with Karl Wendlinger and Heinz-Harald Frentzen, was part of the Mercedes Junior Team, which had been set up to find the best German drivers and coach them into a position where they could enter F1. They were tutored by Jochen Mass and were doing rather well in the Sportscar Championship. 'The Mercedes Junior Team was a good operation geared to find a German star,' said Phillips. 'Though Mercedes were only in sportscars at the time, it was pretty clear F1 was the long-term aim and it was eighteen months later when they bought engine-makers Ilmor in Northampton and started producing engines which they put into the Sauber F1 car. So, probably, Jochen Neerpasch [racing manager at Daimler-Benz and the creator of the Junior Team] knew what the long-term plan was for

Mercedes, but what they needed to do was get a driver with some F1 experience before they took the plunge themselves. So they came to us with a three-year proposal. Schumacher then was a contracted Mercedes Junior Team driver. The deal we were offered was £150,000 per race for 1991, then three million the following year, probably rising to four and a half million for a three-year period. I can't remember the details exactly, but certainly three million for 1992. The caveat was that, if at any time Mercedes entered F1, they would be able to take him back.'

At Spa, Schumacher qualified in seventh place – an astonishing performance as he had never driven around the Ardennes circuit (though it seems the Jordan team were told he had). Except for those few laps at Silverstone, he had never driven an F1 car either. Ahead of him on the grid were Ayrton Senna, Alain Prost, Nigel Mansell, Nelson Piquet, Jean Alesi and Gerhard Berger – a very strong field of drivers, four of them world champions. Schumacher really could not have done any better; for a debutant it was the equivalent of a pole position. His car broke down during the race, but for sure everyone had sat up and noticed what a very few insiders had spotted already.

A sort of feeding frenzy ensued. There are any number of versions of the comings and goings between that Spa race and the next race at Monza. Tales of injunctions, meetings in luxurious lakeside Italian hotels, crossing and double-crossing, and artfully managed media leaks kept the pot boiling for quite some time. In the end Schumacher ended up driving at Monza in the colours of Benetton, then run by

F1 newbie Flavio Briatore, the team for which the German won the first of his world titles. Eddie Jordan was very upset that the *wunderkind* had not stayed: the money paid to the Jordan team would have been good, and of course he would have sold him at a great profit. But he came up against the one man in F1 no one can best.

'Bernie Ecclestone was instrumental in getting him away from us,' said Phillips, 'because he had a piece of information which was our death knell. Schumacher's management were desperate that he should drive a Ford Cosworth, which Benetton were also using, and wanted us to continue using it in 1992.' The trouble for Jordan was that this was not how things were going to pan out in 1992, because a deal had been done before Schumacher had come on to the scene. 'There was only one person at that time who knew we were going to be using Yamaha for the 1992 season. That was Bernie, because he had fixed it for us at the race in Hungary. Indeed, on the Monday after Spa, Eddie was flying to Japan to sign the Yamaha deal. On Sunday morning in Spa I had a conversation with Neerpasch and Willy Weber [Schumacher's manager], and they were talking about the following season and telling me we had to use the Ford engine. "Of course," I said, "yeah, yeah, we will be using the Ford engines," knowing full well we wouldn't be. In that period the Brabham team had Yamaha engines. It wasn't Bernie's any more, but he was still mentoring it, and Herbie Blash was running it. So Bernie was the one person outside our entourage who knew about the change of engines.'

Phillips, who went to public school at Malvern before working his way up at *Autosport* from the status of messenger boy, loves a drink and a joke and is fond of recalling when Ecclestone finally admitted his part in the affair. 'Funnily enough, it was only at Imola in 2006 when I was introducing him to our then new owners. We were talking about drivers, and I said, "Listen, you don't want to bring old drivers in, they are absolutely useless. Jordan is still more famous for introducing Schumacher and other drivers to F1 than ever winning any races." And Bernie piped up, "And then I stole him off you."' Phillips then added another anecdote that again gives the measure of Ecclestone's sense of mischief and timing. 'I remember when I got to Monza [after the Belgian GP, when Schumacher's future was still being contested by the two teams], the first thing I did was to go round to see him to tell him what had been going on. He received me in his old bus where he was poring over some land he had just bought in Sardinia. Once I told him my story he said, "This is absolutely disgraceful. This sort of thing has got to stop." It was only some time later that I pieced it all together and the fact that it was he who had told the Germans, "You can't go there, they'll be running Yamaha next year."'

Phillips said that there were many reasons why Ecclestone steered Schumacher towards Benetton. 'One was that he had just got to know Briatore, who had been around for a year, and wanted to support him. Also, there were no German drivers in F1 at the time, so there was a lot of pressure to put him in the best team possible. There was also the German television station RTL. They too got involved, telling Bernie how much they could do for the sport if Schumacher was successful. And the Yamaha engines were pretty awful. Heavy, big, and a V12 at a time when everyone was moving towards the V10s. It was not the right piece of equipment and it was unreliable. For all of these reasons, Schumacher ended up at Benetton.'

After that, of course, Schumacher soared ever higher and Jordan carried on employing pay drivers to help make ends meet and stay in F1. This has been the fate of a great many teams, in the past 25 years particularly as costs have soared seemingly out of control. If a leading team is budgeting anything between $300 million and $500 million, with the engine provided for free, then the small teams, which have to pay for their engines, must really be up against the wall. In addition, the Concorde Agreement, the contract between the teams and the sport's governing and commercial bodies, allows for substantial financial help for the better-placed teams at the end of each season. In this context, pay drivers become crucial to the ongoing health of the smaller teams, or 'privateers' as Phillips likes to call them.

Phillips observed that, in the 1980s and 1990s, 'Money was not quite as big as it is today. Then, if you asked a driver for a million dollars, that was an awful of money. These days we're talking ten to twelve million euros. The percentage is greater today than it was then. Eddie's mentality when he ran F3 and F3000 teams was that he would always have one or two paying drivers, and they used to sponsor the talent he used to put into his number one car. When he ran Johnny

Herbert and Jean Alesi, people who were good but were not able to pay, Eddie made sure that in the junior categories his second or third cars paid for his first one. That was how we wanted to run F1, by putting a talented person in the top car, not expecting a huge amount of money to come from him, but the second driver would pay quite a bit more. And we never considered paying anyone, though they were paid huge bonuses for points finishes. So, for us at Jordan, in those days, the pay driver operation was not a make-or-break factor for the team. It was useful cash, but not significant in the way Midland, for example, operated. They anticipated that over 50 per cent of their operational costs would come from drivers.' For sure, word in the paddock was that Narain Karthikeyan and Tiago Monteiro had stumped up $10 million each, which paid for the engine supply in 2005 at Jordan/Midland. That, for a small team, is a big headache out of the way. 'A driver like [Robert] Doornbos comes with seven to eight million euros and his backers are basically after passes,' Phillips continued. 'They're not bothered about too much branding. And, as there is not much to choose between him and Tonio Liuzzi at Toro Rosso, you can see which way the management may be tempted to go.'

The truth is that everyone who gets to F1 is a pay driver, especially in the early part of their career. A sponsor or motor manufacturer can always bring influence to bear to get them started; there are very few who don't pay anything along the line. It is very common to hear team managers, journalists and, of course, agents discussing young drivers and arranging test drives for their protégés. This is how the paddock works, constantly dealing with the placing of young drivers. For example, in 2005 a fledgling GP2 team went to see Ecclestone to ask for advice and guidance on how best to start the team. Mr E listened to their presentation then told them they could choose one of their drivers, but the other should be Robert Kubica, the fast Polish karting phenomenon who had just won himself a test drive with Renault in F1. In the end, the chips fell differently.

Still, some of the big teams are shy of experimenting with rookies and would rather pay tens of millions of dollars for tried and tested drivers. 'Look at Honda,' Phillips pointed out. 'Eighty-odd million dollars for Button over five years and thirty million for three years of Barrichello's services. This is nonsense! It would be nice to think that the manufacturers or the team could nurture talent. It would be a great thing to be able to do, but, from a privateer's point of view, it is just not possible. We do not have that kind of excess budget. Renault and Flavio have done very well, using Renault money. He puts young drivers on long-term contracts and guarantees them drives for the junior categories all the way to F1. And they are paid – a small amount of money – and they are well taught. McLaren have done it with [Lewis] Hamilton. You can invest in these guys and when you bring them into F1 you have them relatively cheaply. If you want to buy a star it will cost you tens of millions, but, if you have homegrown ones, you are calling the shots and getting your investment back.

'Privateers act as talent spotters,' Phillips continued. 'It's
the role we have to play. The big teams do not take the
chance. In 2006 Frank Williams did take a chance by putting
young [Nico] Rosberg in the car, but that was probably
pressure from Keke, which is pretty irresistible. I imagine
Frank is sitting there thinking he has only finished two
races, and dropped down to eighth in the championship –
the worst Williams have ever been in 25 years, I think. No
money changes hands, as far as I know, but it turned out to
be a disastrous year and it will put him off running a rookie
again. From our point of view we can't buy talent, so we
have to bring the new boys on. If we spot one early enough,
and we write a good enough contract, we will be able to sell
him on, as we did in the old days with [Eddie] Irvine and
[Jean] Alesi. We made good money from them.' Phillips
added that lots of drivers don't like the stigma of being
called pay drivers. 'But it's a fact of life and it's your way in,
and if you're good enough you get out of it. After three
years, if you've done a decent job as an apprentice, you can
expect to get paid. But you have to be good enough.'

But of course having often very rich young men
effectively in charge of the fortunes of hundreds of employees
is not an easy task for the team management. 'First and
foremost you have to treat them as an employee,' Phillips
explained, 'and therefore they should be accountable at all
times for their actions: you have to drive the car, you have to
go to press conferences, you have to do any number of
sponsor days throughout the year, you have to keep yourself
fit. The guys have to be accountable to the team on a number

of different levels, so you've got to be their boss and try to make sure they perform their job to the absolute best of their ability. But the big problem with a paying driver is you can't really call the shots. They're paying us for the privilege of driving. You can advise them that they should be fitter and that there are certain things they've got to do, but they tend not to. The worst thing about most drivers is their complete and utter disregard for fitness. There are certain ones who do the business, but most of them, no. I think they go through a little bit of fitness training in the winter. They go skiing in January and come back fairly fit, but you listen to them in the car, on the radio, and they're huffing and puffing. It's not on really, but it is mighty difficult when they're paying you ten million quid to be too hard on them. Those are your terms of employment, however, and you ought to be accountable.

'Obviously the teams that employ their drivers can do things differently. The system Briatore set up [at Renault] is terrific. They've got this health and wellbeing centre, which is not just for the drivers, it's also for employees, which I think is a bloody good thing. Some people see it as a luxury, but, to be honest, without your health you've got nothing. And don't forget we do a lot of travelling which is pretty stressful and tiring. Typically you shrug off ailments, you think you'll sort them out, and, of course, you don't.

'I'm a great believer that drivers should be treated as employees. Getting them to come here to the factory is usually a painful experience, though to be fair we don't really have it with the two we have now [at Spyker, Monteiro and Albers], but one or two we've had over the years would have been mystery men if they'd turned up here. Nobody would have known who they were. It was shocking. OK, give them the day off, but then they should be here on the Tuesday after a race or, if they're testing, on the Thursday. There are two hundred guys here working all hours. It's not just the people who go racing, it's the factory staff. There's a lot of people involved, working mightily unsocial hours, and for them to turn up on the Thursday afternoon at a push – well, it's scandalous. I have to say, whether we're Jordan, Midland, whatever, the drivers have been near enough allowed to get away with murder, and I'm not sure whether other teams are like that. Rubens [Barrichello] was OK because he lived locally, but if they're living in a tax haven somewhere, they don't want to be in the UK. Any excuse not to be here.'

Jo Ramirez has been in world championship-winning teams as well as smaller ones, and has seen how the pay driver world has evolved. 'There's not so many of them now because there are not so many small teams,' he observed. 'I suppose you could say Christian Klien got the Red Bull Racing drive because of his Red Bull connections. Sometimes there are gentleman drivers who like to do it. They can afford it, so why not? Like Pedro Diniz, who drove the Prost. He was not a bad driver, and he had the best motor home in the paddock, so he was always very welcome. There were others, like Elio de Angelis. When he first started, he was helped by his father's construction company, but he also was a good driver, he also had the passion. Then you have other drivers like Hector Rebaque from Mexico. He didn't do badly, but I think it was probably his father had the passion more than him. He didn't really apply himself otherwise he probably could have gone up from a pay driver to be being a paid driver, but I think his father was pushing him. And there have been others who have been a waste of time, like Ricardo Simeno. Some of these pay drivers race with the family money, like Rebaque and Diniz, but there are other drivers who manage instead to get enough money from a sponsor from their country, like Jos Verstappen or Jan Lammers. These are the better kinds of pay drivers to have. They have already shone in all the formulae, they are racers, and they are very committed.'

Rebaque is an interesting case. Not only was he a pay driver but, when he couldn't get a drive, he wouldn't be dissuaded from joining the F1 circus. After an unsuccessful year with Hesketh in 1978 he bought an ex-factory Lotus and formed his own team. He did the same the year after. His best result was sixth in the German GP. After that he moved up a notch and decided to commission Penske to build him his own F1 car. He didn't have much success with that, but surely he has managed to be the ultimate pay driver.

I asked Ramirez about the eternal balancing act the team must perform in accepting drivers with money who could easily nullify the incoming finances by crashing the car into a wall. 'It's a tight decision,' he said. 'Very often it's close, and you do have crashes. I remember one time we had a small insurance on the car, but the premiums are so expensive it's never worth doing it. This is why many drivers start with a budget year because there's a chance they won't finish. Pay drivers sometimes feel that they don't get a fair crack of the whip, especially when their team-mate is paid. They then feel they are the ones bringing in the money, and this money is to help the other driver, their team-mate.

'It's getting harder and harder now, though. For a start you need to have a super licence [which proves you can drive at a high level]. In the past it was much easier, but I guess if you have been good enough in other formulae to persuade a big company to have faith in you, to put money in you, it's a legitimate way to get into F1. A lot of drivers have come that way. Like Senna: he was helped hugely by the National Bank in Brazil [the Nacional] and he always stayed very loyal to them, even when the bank had problems and they couldn't pay him enough. "They helped me when I needed them most," he would say. That was the type of man he was.'

My only real experience of interacting with a pay driver (family money) was with Paolo Barilla – and by 'interacting' I mean away from the usual bland media exchanges that characterise pay drivers' stays in F1. (Ironically, it is easier to establish a relationship with one of the 'bigger' drivers simply because they will be around for longer and will provide the best copy; pay drivers tend to get sidelined by the media pack as a result.) Barilla was the heir of a bakery and pasta empire in the cash-rich city of Parma, a family business that had started in the mid-nineteenth century. It had proved very successful and had created great wealth: the Barilla family's modern painting collection, including works by Miró, Picasso, Chagall and Braque, is one of the world's best. Paolo Barilla started in karting, like so many other F1 drivers, then graduated through F3 and F2, where he bagged a drive with Minardi alongside Alessandro Nannini, another future F1 driver. In 1985 he managed to win at Le Mans, and two years later was a Benetton test driver. A year after that, in Japan, and while a spectator in civilian clothing, he very bravely rescued a Danish driver from a burning wreck. Then came a spell as Minardi test driver, and finally regular driver in 1990. But, at the end of that season, Giancarlo Minardi replaced him with Gianni Morbidelli, and that was effectively the end of Barilla's F1 career.

Barilla was good-looking, affable, with no airs or graces about him, despite his gilded background. I once asked him if he could drive me round a lap of Spa so that I could do an old-fashioned reporter's job and write about what it felt like to be driven around this fearsome circuit.

Frank Williams used to position himself at the bottom of Eau Rouge (before it was watered down) and just watch the cars along the back straight speeding towards the hill leading up to the left- and right-hander. You could hear which drivers 'lifted' and which kept the pedal to the metal, and you could see how the cars behaved. Indeed, you could tell a lot about a driver from that vantage point. At the time Sir Frank told me, 'It takes courage, and of course you must trust your car too. And it takes a lot of stomach.' I know it does, because I also drove up and round Eau Rouge, not in what was then a 700hp monster machine, but in a little Opel Corsa.

Barilla, you see, was more than happy to drive me round Spa, so after practice we met and went looking for one of the team's road cars. He was after the Mercedes he had been given for the weekend, but someone was using it. So, after much head scratching and apologies, he was given the keys of this resplendent blue Opel Corsa 1.2. I was mentally picturing the face of my sports editor at the *Sunday Times*, who had been enthused by the idea of a first-hand piece with a racing driver careering at top speed around this iconic circuit. I didn't think an Opel Corsa 1.2 would float his boat, as it were. Still, there I was, getting into this family runabout on a damp, drizzly day and listening to Barilla telling me to strap in tightly.

What followed was an experience that has stayed with me all these years, as clear as when it was happening. The first thing I realised was that this young man was quite brilliant behind the wheel. No amount of TV watching or reading can prepare you for the sheer skill level all F1 drivers possess. As Jackie Stewart explained at the beginning of this book, F1 drivers are the best of the best, and Barilla was at the time in F1. That he was a pay driver, a very rich young man able to indulge his passion, was not really relevant. He was still good enough to drive the hell out of the Opel Corsa 1.2 around Spa and always to stay in complete control, playing the car like a musical instrument.

He also had time to run a commentary for me. Every single bump, indentation and kerb was highlighted, explained and analysed. As we hit the dip before the Eau Rouge hill at about 70mph, as opposed to the more usual

160mph, my heart jumped into my mouth and my backside took quite a hit as the little car bottomed out. What it must feel like in an F1 car I can only guess. Then it was up the hill, just recovering from the compression as Barilla hurtled us over the top. And on he went, all the way round. As I had hardly managed to write anything down first time round, Barilla took me round again. More slithering and sliding, more bumping and grinding, and all the way through Barilla was calm, in control, well within his comfort zone.

In a way, Barilla had nothing to lose – a bit of fun in F1, then back to the family business. But other pay drivers are a little more frantic, and they make it their business to have pushy managers. These managers don't always act in their charges' best interests, as Ian Phillips told me. 'You have to have a little bit of experience in dealing with the managers,' he said. 'Some you know are not going to waste your time, because they don't just take on all and sundry. Flavio's generally got someone who's good, Enrico Zanarini's normally got somebody who's good, Willy Weber's normally got somebody who's good, but the rest you have to take as you find them, and you've just got to go through the whole system, test them out. Of course, if a manager's being paid, you realise he's got to talk up his client. The guys who are coming to us, they're not going to get a wage. He will be paid somewhere along the line, though, and, yes, always with the proviso that you know they're pushing a client they're being paid for. Generally we would know a driver's background and how good they really are, but you've got to listen to everybody, because sometimes you just don't know. You've got to understand the circumstances that they've been through, but there are those who come up with all the list of excuses. At the end of the day you've got to be ruthless about it. The decision will always be balanced by the sort of budget you might have available. But you've got to listen to them all.

'Sponsors or potential sponsors all say the same thing: they always tell you in July that they've got £10 million to spend, and, if we could just give them passes for a weekend at Monza, which is two weeks before budgets are signed off, then they can make the deal happen. So you give them the weekend at Monza, and you'll probably never see them again, because they've had that for free. The golden rule is, any prospective sponsor has to come and have a day at Silverstone testing before he goes anywhere near a race. That means that during the week they've got to take a day off work and, if they're genuine, somebody will know they're taking a day off work to come and talk about it. But if they go to Monza on Saturday and Sunday nobody in their company needs to know.

'Many drivers are advised by journalists. I used to do it in the old days for not a penny. They can make the introductions, see it through, and make sure an Eddie Jordan or a Colin Kolles [team principal of Midland F1, now known as Spyker] gets to know who these people are, and in turn the teams keep an eye on what these drivers are up to, as Eddie and I used to do in the early days. Weekends when we weren't at a Grand Prix, we were watching F3 races or F3000 races, and I know how frustrating it is in the junior classes: they're at Thruxton with two men and a dog watching and there's actually nobody taking any interest from the F1 side. And a father is paying half a million a year and wondering how on earth do they get some attention. GP2 is now delivering in this area. It's a good format, the racing is good, and people are actually watching it.

'You've got to know the manager network, so you know who you can trust. I know most of us – and we always did under Eddie – keep an eye on the results in other parts of the world, because eventually you will get a call from somebody, "I represent so-and-so". I think it's discourteous not to know what it is they've been doing. I think it's part of our business to have the finger on the pulse. As it happens, it's a very enjoyable aspect of the job, because when you find somebody good it's very rewarding, it really is. That's the function of the smaller independent teams right now, and that's what we've got to do.'

Finally a thought from Flavio Briatore, who is, after Bernie Ecclestone, the most powerful man in F1 by virtue of his extraordinary achievements, his vision and a refreshing streak of eccentricity. 'Never seen a rich kid who was fast, never,' he stated. 'They just don't have the hunger. And even if they are fast, well, when I see twenty-year-olds with the Porsche and three mobile phones, I don't even bother to look at them. I know they are not going to make it. I think we should look at these super licences. Some of these guys shouldn't be driving on a normal road, forget about a racetrack.'

CHAPTER FIVE

MANAGING THE TALENT

Pay drivers may need managers but of course all drivers need managing, from the moment they show promise in karting to when they sign the big-money deal that will set them up for life.

The manager is a complex figure. In F1 they are not regulated in any way, and they come from all sides of the paddock. Some are former journalists, others come from athlete management agencies. There is a smattering of lawyers and accountants. Some are team principals or former drivers, others are friends, fathers or other members of the family. Some drivers trust their hometown lawyers, others go for the big agencies, or set up their own. In short, it is a varied world, and the drivers need as much skill and luck to find the right manager as they do for driving.

Martin Brundle is one of these managers. A former driver with 158 Grand Prix starts and a Le Mans winner as well, he is now a television commentator and a columnist as well as a driver manager, in partnership with his friend and fellow driver Mark Blundell. If there is a conflict of interest of any kind, Brundle is not aware of one. This is very much how F1 works, as much is still taken on trust. Insiders are accepted; it takes time for outsiders to get to that point.

'There are about 30 decision-makers in the paddock who decide who is going to drive,' Brundle said. 'What you try to do is build a picture, and it is remarkably easy to find out how long drivers' contracts are, how long the options are, so that you can build this picture as to where slots might open. There are a few surprises of course, like Alonso going to McLaren, which did take the market by surprise, but generally everything is well flagged up.' Brundle then explained the process of introducing someone into F1, and once more the figure of the pay driver came to the fore. 'Of course it helps if you can come in with a sponsor supporting you,' he said. 'Question is, does coming in with a sponsor make you a pay driver? I cannot think of any pay driver transferring to fully paid-up legendary F1 driver. It seems to be a stigma you cannot get rid of. But the bottom line is that if you are really special you will do it. I have always said that I do not know any driver who should have been in an F1 car but wasn't. There's only one exception in the 24 years I've been involved, and that's Tomas Kristensen, who went on to become a six-time Le Mans winner. Anyone else I know at some point had a chance. Might have not made the grade at the time, for whatever reason, but he had the chance. But if you paint him as a pay driver, then he'll spend his whole career as a pay driver. It is very difficult, if not impossible, to come in as a pay driver and go out a paid driver. And it is true that a lot of kids come into F1 with debt round their neck.'

Mark Webber, though he would be delighted to be described as a kid, is someone who knows about debt and the role played by managers in that context. 'In the lower formulae, in many cases it's up to the drivers to fund the teams and its personnel,' he said. 'And coming up through the lower categories, the feedback from the sponsors is so small. The point is, it costs £350,000 to drive in F3, and there is no return on the investment. It is purely a labour of love for those who are paying for it. I had a lot of that from Stoddy [Paul Stoddart] and Flavio [Briatore]. Both supported me to the hilt. In 2001 I owed Stoddy £750,000 for helping me, which included a test drive for Tom Walkinshaw's Arrows. I had to pay him back or give him a percentage of my F1 earnings. Flavio took over the debt, told me not to worry about it. He gave me the Renault test drive, then placed me at Minardi, then Jordan, then Williams, and now Red Bull Racing. He is a great guy and I owe him a lot. I won't have a bad word said about him. He resurrected my career and positioned me for my career to grow.'

Briatore's most famous charge is Fernando Alonso. When the two of them were at Renault there appeared to be something of a conflict of interest, but no one seemed to be bothered. Indeed, the paddock considers the Italian to be at the top of his game, which he very clearly is. He manages his drivers through a separate company and says he is always on the lookout for new talent. 'I have a good structure in place which looks out for young drivers. I have managed the interests of Fisichella, Trulli, Webber, Alonso and, of course, Schumacher. After I discovered Michael, I had many young drivers write to me. Before that they were much older, but I had my group of managers evaluate the young ones who came to me. You must be on top of the drivers. They must know you are there – there to solve problems, to help them and be positive. The relationship must be transparent. After all, these guys are travelling at 300kph [188mph]; there is no room for funny games. You get a feeling for these guys, and I spend a fair amount of time with them. You have to be on top of things. Of course I have made mistakes, but I would say my strike rate is high – Schumi, Fisi, Trulli, Webber, Alonso, and now [Heikki] Kovalainen. Webber has been with me since 2001. I bought him out of his contract with Stoddart ... can't remember whether it was 1.5 million euros or pounds. Other teams do it differently, they buy the talent in, for huge amounts of money. [Ron] Dennis bought Raikkonen for $30 million from Sauber. I don't agree with this. You must invest; the world is not one big blank chequebook. Look at Real Madrid – what a disaster. You have to be efficient in your job and take the right decisions. When I got rid of Button to sign Alonso, the British press really murdered me. I can still remember the articles. I told them, "Only the future will be the judge of my decision." Now, what happened to Alonso, and what happened to Button?'

Phillips and a number of other paddock insiders agree with Briatore. They regard the development of drivers as a responsibility of the teams and something that can help young drivers get their chance earlier. 'What is happening now is that some young drivers have leapfrogged the system, like [Sebastian] Vettel with BMW,' Martin Brundle observed. 'We used to have young driver programmes, at Marlboro, Elf, Camel, and that was quite restrictive. Take the Elf Pilotage programme – only [Olivier] Panis got through. The problem is that if we carry a particular flag, we are restricting the possibilities by aiming at such a tight range of opportunities to drive F1 cars. And if you are already carrying a sponsor's badge with you, it limits you even further. It's the same with the Red Bull driver programme or the Toyota or Renault programmes. On the other hand, a bit like snakes and ladders, it gives young drivers a fantastic opportunity to go up the ladder. But there are the snakes too, and it saddens me to see so many drivers arriving with so much baggage. The F3 team owners saw it a while back: the F1 megastar, earning millions, will pass through their team a few years earlier, and these kids are being taken out of the marketplace, as far back as karting. They want to nail them down as early as possible. There is a series of legal restrictions on how early you can nail a driver. The Robbos [David and Steve Robertson], I respect them, because they invested hard cash in Kimi and Button and hit the jackpot twice. Many will see them earning significant amounts of money and with quite a powerful base, but they are the template if you are not running a funded, structured driver training programme.

'How many driver managers do you know in this paddock? There are so few. And who would you trust? Who do you know who can knock on any door and walk right in? We are very unpopular. I am in a strange position as I do the media and I do all sorts of things. I drove for seven of these teams, and I helped DC [David Coulthard] out as a mate, and I'm very pleased to say he is still a mate, very much a mate, but the teams hate us. They need us, and hate us. All we are ever going to do is cost them money and chew their ears off. But at the same time you have to have someone to do their smelly stuff, because the team boss and the driver want to have certain relationships. The smelly stuff needs to be done with a third party, which the team bosses despise, and then watch him eat his food and drink his coffee for the rest of the year in their hospitality, which they hate. And then the agent is going to bust their balls again at the end of the year. It's quite a funny process.'

Brundle then highlighted what a small window of opportunity managers have to show off their clients to the few teams in F1. 'Luckily, cream rises to the top,' he said. 'What Mark [Blundell] and I have to do is bring them to the attention of the right people. These are busy people, they are running $400 million teams, they make the big decisions and they don't have the time to soak all the info up. They need bringing up to speed, and to be told where the talent is. Once it is in front of them, they can soon spot it. They know what they are looking for. When you plug that kid in the car, he usually has just one shot to make it happen.' It's a tough call, Brundle reckons. One shot is not much, but 'they've been at it since the age of eight. DC was one of the first of the professional racing drivers; they haven't done anything else since the age of eight, earlier in some cases. They have always raced. In some ways they have no reality check; they have been groomed to be racing drivers. All they have done is race, train, prepare. A kid like Vettel, you stick him in and he hits the ground running. It's just extraordinary. It has all changed dramatically. The drivers seem to be younger and younger.

Brundle also feels that he has to keep a special eye on his young charges, much more than in the past, which means he strays into the realm of in loco parentis. 'It becomes a very individual relationship,' he said. 'The chemistry can work in different ways. Carrot, stick, kick up the arse, advice – it all depends on the person. Some need a hug, others a kick. And there is a huge element missing: they don't have a proper life. Where do they draw from when they have a dip? Where is their inner core of strength? So I think this is where the manager comes in, to give them a reality check.'

Like all driver managers and senior team management, Didier Coton, too, is always on the lookout for new talent. And, he told me, the scouting process is by no means streamlined or structured. 'It's word of mouth; it's contacts. Very often I've been approached by people who've said, "This driver is looking for an agent, a manager, would you like to see him?" and I say, "OK, let's have a talk." Or you look a little bit in different racing series to see what's going on, who's doing what, why this one is so special. The selection process is pretty wide; it can come from anywhere and different kinds of opportunities. After that, once you have identified a potential driver to take on, you still need to decide whether you will take him on or not. That will be answered by seeing his results, but most especially after meeting him. You need to feel a current between two people. If you feel comfortable when you speak with him, if you feel the guy has what it takes and is prepared to sacrifice enormously, then it's something, and you start to warm to him. If the current doesn't flow, it's not worth continuing.'

As we know from chapter 1, the Belgian manager feels that he too has grown into the kind of operator who believes his charges must have the complete package to be considered by the teams. He is acutely aware of what a modern Grand Prix driver has to bring to a team. 'Because Formula One has become more and more technical, the driver has to learn from a younger age, and as they grow into the system. There is much bigger technology now at every level, in aerodynamics, with the engine, but also with computer skills, because all the software is analysed, the car is full of sensors, and so on. For a driver nowadays, just being quick is not good enough. He has to be able to work with the engineers, who in many ways are the team's "doctors". If a driver gives them a wrong feeling, or information, for what's happening in the car, the engineer, the doctor, will diagnose incorrectly and prescribe the wrong cure. So young drivers need to have a great feeling for the car, and they also need to be able to analyse the computer readings. The driver who doesn't spend time with the technical side of the job of being an F1 driver will very quickly feel lost. For me it is vital nowadays that young drivers start working as soon as possible on the technical skills they have and get more and more interested in how the car is built, how the telemetry works, how he can solve problems, how he can find things out. If you don't have an interest in this you're not going to be a complete driver.'

Coton's role is a lot more hands-on than it used to be. 'Different companies, different managers, operate differently. Some are just doing a contract for them – "thank you very much". Personally, I do everything for them. Whatever needs to be done is done. If they travel a long way and will be away for two weeks, we look after their apartments, we look after their financial things, just to make sure we can say, "Guys, get on the plane, see you in two weeks, and when you come back everything will be fine. If there's anything you think about, make sure you make a list, and I want this list by Wednesday because by Thursday you're at the track and I don't want you thinking about it. I'll see you on Monday, or I'll see you at the track, or whatever." Everything has to be done because, compared to any other sport, your mind needs to be free [to race in F1]. We're in Monaco today, and here, when you are driving, you do one thing wrong, a little mistake, you go into the Armco and that is the end of the race. All that time, effort and planning is wasted. So you need to provide performance, as we are all searching for the thousands of tenths of a second to be the first to get an advantage. You can only do that if you have a strong and clear mind.'

But Coton also reminds me that good driver management is about simple things, everyday details that apply to just about anything in life. 'There are a lot of things I explain to young drivers that are taken from normal life: how to eat properly, how to do this, how to do that. It's the logical things you would educate your own family to do. When you take a driver, you take him for the long term, and he'll have to go through all this as if we were a family, an extra one to theirs and mine. Sometimes they become part of my family, sometimes I'm part of theirs. That's what you need to do. You need to have a very, very strong relationship so that they don't hide anything from you. You must understand everything, but also they must understand what I want, how I want it, and the way I operate. If those things match, you have a fantastic foundation to work from, and then you can really progress. I speak with my guys once a day, minimum, all of them. Remember, they're under a lot of pressure. They work with a team that is basically their employer. They're very relaxed with them because they have a good relationship with the team, but they need somebody to whom they can explain everything openly, outside the team environment. You also need to have a good understanding of the person to recognise when he has a dip in performance, if he has the flu, what else might be wrong. I need to be in a position to help, and that will come through experience and the fact that you are communicating with them a lot of the time. That's the bottom line – you need to speak with them frequently – and that's the way I operate.'

Perhaps the most extreme test of the relationship between manager and driver comes after a major shunt, at which time the manager must perform a vital role in terms of healing and recovery, and media and sponsor management. I can clearly remember when Mika Hakkinen had his big accident in Adelaide, during Friday qualifying for the 1995 Australian GP. His left rear tyre deflated suddenly and, after hitting a kerb and being spun in the air, he hit the wall side-on at about 120mph, suffering an estimated impact of 150G. There were fears for his life during the fifteen minutes the medical team took to stabilise him at trackside before allowing him to be driven away in the ambulance. I wasn't at the circuit, but I was woken up in the UK soon after it had happened by my assistant at McLaren, who, clearly deeply shaken, wanted guidance on what to do in media terms. All teams have, or should have, a media disaster strategy, and we talked through it. Meanwhile the team was quite literally shutting down, going within itself in order to cope better. This is what McLaren had also done after Ayrton Senna's accident in 1994. TV sets in the garages were turned off. The team must stay focused on the job. It is, in this sense, a military outlook.

Thankfully, the Finnish driver made a wonderful recovery, though Coton, in his modest way, is reluctant to speak of these times. 'I won't explain too much because it's a very private thing,' he said, 'but the first thing that comes to your mind is how he is, because you don't know until you get [news] from the doctors. The first reaction is, of course, what is happening, how is he? That's when you understand the condition he is in. Then it becomes something you can't force; you need to let the healing process run itself. It is a question of time, and time is not something you can rush or catch up on. Rushing a sportsman to get back on his feet would be a mistake. Give him space, let him recover on his own, let the body re-establish its own patterns of behaviour, and let his mind do the same. When all that starts to happen, then you come to the point when you need to start speaking about things. But you mustn't say, "Are you going to be fit for racing? What do you want to do?" This is the guaranteed way to destroy your relationship with your driver and, anyway, it will get you nowhere. The only man who will decide where he wants to go, even if he wants to have a drive again, is the driver. "Call me when you're ready," I told him. And one day he did, to say he'd like to try again. That's how it works. He got back in the car and won two world championships.

'Any sportsman can have an accident. You have to let the time pass and let the person recover. Sportsmen at this level are extremely fit individuals, and this means they are able to recover very quickly. Sometimes the speed of recovery borders on the incredible. With Mika, the McLaren team was absolutely phenomenal. And that's everybody: the sponsors, the team itself, the team principal – nobody was trying to force the issue. But the most important thing when accidents like this happen is the private life: the family, his wife. Everybody was there for him. If you're lucky enough to have the right environment around you, it's going to be fine. But if you have people who don't understand, you may never recover.'

Having said that, Coton added that Hakkinen was incredibly strong mentally and there was never a need for any kind of psychological support, in a professional sense. 'Mika never expressed a wish for that. He managed to do it on his own.' I wondered at this ability to cope with what must have been a terrifying experience, on a number of levels. Physically, of course, but mentally and emotionally too. Racing drivers are a breed apart, and this is most apparent in these situations. Most people would experience flashbacks and cold sweats each and every time they got near a car after an accident like that. Not Mika, and not the long and distinguished line of drivers before him who have had a mighty off. 'Most of them are like that,' Coton continued. 'They manage to analyse things very quickly and say to themselves, "That's the way it is." There is no panic, nothing untoward; they are cool under pressure. They can sustain pressure very well – it's incredible the way they do that. Racing drivers have a way of blocking their mind. It's a very interesting process. They may have a big off, then get back in the car ten minutes later and do the qualifying time. These guys anticipate an awful lot; they know exactly what's going to happen. They simply say to themselves, "OK, it's gone, I lost it that time." That is how it works. They know how to react. If you know what may be about to happen, you think more about protecting yourself – simple self-preservation – than worry about too many feelings.'

As Martin Brundle mentioned, the relationship between the teams and the managers can also be a delicate one. The very make-up of the F1 paddock, with all the motor homes tightly squeezed in a long line along one side, and all the trucks backing into the pits on the other side, makes it difficult for outsiders to find a place to rest their feet. And managers are often considered to be outsiders by a number of the teams: they are not part of the pit crew, they are not in marketing or PR, and they are not involved in sponsor relations, all of whom have some office or desk space assigned to them in the motor homes. Then there are the catering staff, and of course the team management. Modern motor homes may be palatial by yesteryear's standards, but they are still limited in space, so managers have to find a precarious perch in 'their' motor home, from where their driver operates, or wander up and down the paddock – the shark pool – doing the walk and the talk while constantly looking around to see if there is someone more important to speak to. Thus the manager has to manage the team too, so that he and his charge are operating in the best possible environment.

Coton is an easy-going man, a character trait that helps him when it comes to his relationships with the teams. 'I never had any problem with the teams,' he said. 'I try to provide them with what they are looking for so the driver is ready to achieve the performance they're looking for and to have minimum problems with that. We try to collaborate with them more than anything else and make their life easier, because they are busy. The marketing and press departments are very busy, so we try to help them make a good schedule with the drivers, to make sure the driver is there on time and does the job. That's the only thing they ask. The relationship can be great in negotiation, but that's a different story. The job of an agent, I think, is more to help the team, and also to protect the driver. You have to make sure you don't end up with a crazy schedule. We never say no to promotion or press work, but we do sometimes ask if we could revise it. We try to point out that maybe a big interview done at a certain time is not going to work, as the journalist will have only ten minutes to work with and will therefore not be happy about it. And the driver too is going to answer in very short sentences because his mind won't be on it. In the end it's only a question of compromise, which is why we never turn down an interview request. Promotional work works in a similar way. We look at his schedule. He has to go to this Grand Prix, then do a promotional appearance somewhere totally different, then he has to go testing, so we say, "Hold on a minute, what are you looking for?" It's a question of working together and trying to make sure that both parties, the drivers and the teams, are happy with the schedule, and then when all this is done to everyone's satisfaction, the driver can still be in good shape to perform his primary job.

'Most of the teams my drivers have worked for have been absolutely fantastic for those drivers. I've never had experience of a team principal not being absolutely behind the driver and providing everything he needs to be comfortable and to be able to perform at the highest level. And teams are really big nowadays. There are a lot of very different people in there doing many, many jobs, and the driver is one of the elements. An important one, of course, because he's at the end of the chain, which means he's a vital factor. When you put all this investment in the hands of a driver, it is clear any team principal would try to make sure the guy has everything he needs to perform. If a team fronts up and provides him with everything he needs and he doesn't perform, that's when sometimes a problem can arise. This would mean that one of my drivers isn't sacrificing enough, he's not working hard enough. I'll be the first one to sit down with him and say, "What are you doing? What do you think you are playing at?" Because the job they do on the track also reflects on you as a manager.'

Coton's memories of his years with Mika Hakkinen when both were learning their trade are revealing, for both sides of the relationship. 'I started with world champion Keke Rosberg who basically explained to me how the system works. I worked with him for ten years and I learnt a lot from him. He is a great guy. A fantastic driver, of course, but also a great manager. He had two drivers at the time, and one of them was Mika. When Mika started to move up the big ladder with a top team, McLaren, Keke felt he needed somebody with him full-time. It was very good for me as Mika is a very demanding driver – not because he's a star, but because he's very precise with everything he does, and he teaches you to go into detail too. Very often we would be talking together and he'd say to me, "Let's think about the negatives. How can we do better?" I'd say, "What do you mean 'we'?" He'd say, "How can I do better, how can you do better? Do we need to change something?" By saying that frequently, it pushes you constantly. Every morning now I think "How can I do better?" It's very rare to have drivers like this and you learn a lot from them. Don't forget, he's been world champion twice. You don't become world champion just like that. Every single parameter outside the car has to be perfect first. I use the same kind of formula to train the young ones today, to make sure they understand they have to be absolutely at the top with everything they do, because it works. I was very fortunate and lucky to work with Keke at the time and then to end up with Mika. I'm managing him again right now. The relationship is ongoing for fifteen years – never a row, never a dispute, never an argument. I am proud that I've never had an argument with any of my drivers.'

In the previous chapter, Ian Phillips remarked on how important the way a driver behaves is to the well-being of the team, and how many of these sportsmen can either be rude to or uncaring about all the people who are involved in getting them to the racetrack and keeping them on it. 'You need to explain to them the importance of being part of a team, and the importance of every single member of that team,' said Phillips. 'The mechanic, the cook – everyone matters, from the lower levels to the highest. And they need to understand that when the car goes off, when they damage the car, there's guys who will stay up till three in the morning fixing it for them, so that they will be able to race again. That deserves respect. Personally I have no problem with my guys. They all have a high degree of respect for the mechanics, the engineers, and the people in the motor home who are there from five in the morning serving breakfast with a smile, and who then close the motor home at one in the morning with the same smile. My job is to get this right from the beginning, as they move up racing categories, with the teams getting bigger: you need to understand it's 50, then it's 100, then it's 600 [employees], and you need to be able to go to the factory, to go to every department and say, "Hi, how are you?" It's time-consuming, but they're all working with an end product and they need to understand that. That's teamwork. You need to have it to motivate everybody. I always tell my drivers, "Those guys work with you, not for you. Don't ever forget that."'

So managers are most certainly not bag carriers, though some bag carriers think they are managers. Managers are a bit of everything, but one of the key points is that they very much act as brokers between their clients (the drivers) and the teams that employ them. The relationship is a little different if dealing with a pay driver, but the essentials of selection, mentoring and looking for financial backing are constant. Beyond that, as Phillips and Coton mentioned, it is down to personal relationships, where track record and as much honesty as is possible in the ever-shifting sands of F1 come at a premium and are therefore much prized.

CHAPTER SIX

FIT TO SIT

It has happened to all of us who work in motor racing, and F1 in particular, at a dinner party, or in the pub. 'Easy money these guys earn in F1. No more big accidents and, let's face it, they're just driving around. OK, it's faster than what I normally drive at, but how hard can it be? It's their job after all. Easy money. They're just sitting there, changing the gears quicker than I can. Big deal. Then, at the end, they get out of the car, spray a little champagne about the place, and go home in their private plane. Just look at a football player, look how tired he is after a game. No, it's not a real sport. With a bit of practice anyone could do it.' This, or a variation thereof, I have heard for years and years. It gets to the point where I try not to disclose what world I work in: the person I am talking to will be either a super fan who knows more than I will ever know, or totally scathing about the sport, the people involved, and the drivers in particular.

But it is a tough sport, and the drivers are very fit young men – mentally, as we have seen, and physically too. F1 is peculiar, it is true, in the sense that they are sitting down to do their job. The nearest comparison is probably a jockey, astride a powerful horse that has a mind of its own and on occasion uses it to devastating effect. But in horse racing the danger is more apparent and immediate. Jockeys are a lot more visible, and the pulsating energy of the horse, its bulging muscles, the strain on the riders' faces – all are captured live on television. You can almost feel yourself straining, pulling on the reins, squeezing with your knees. In short, you can participate, you can empathise. And, at the end, the jockeys look as if they have done a tiring, dangerous thing. Not so with racing drivers. Ironically, it is their high level of fitness that disguises the tiredness and strain induced by driving a race car on the limit. In the old days they had big forearms and dust rings round their eyes, or they looked shagged out, as James Hunt often did. The point is, they were tired, as they had wrestled hard with the car, track and opponents. It was gladiatorial. Nowadays drivers seem to aspire to Michael Schumacher's Zen-like calm immediately after the race, in a fit state to conduct multilingual interviews in a cool, calm and collected way, not a bead of sweat to be seen anywhere.

But it really is a tough sport, and a challenging environment to be operating in. Gary Harstein is the FIA's medical delegate, which means he is the person in charge of all things medical at every F1 Grand Prix (he has followed on from Professor Sid Watkins, the British neurosurgeon who was originally tasked with setting up on-track medical facilities – essentially a compact A&E unit – at every race on the calendar). A genial Brussels-based American, he brings to the paddock a wry sense of humour. He knows exactly why drivers have to be fit sportsmen: careering around racetracks at great speeds is not really what the human body was designed for. The upper body and the neck are the two areas most subject to G-forces, and therefore most in need of strength and conditioning. By way of explanation, 1G is the earth's gravitational pull, so one could say that is one's body weight. At 5G, then, a 75kg racing driver will be experiencing five times his body weight – some 375kg. The space shuttle pulls 3G at take-off; F1 drivers can and do experience higher loads over and over again as they go round corners on the racetracks.

'Most of the G-forces are going to get absorbed in most of the lower body by the extremely form-fitting seats and the tight belts where they're not moving their body around very much,' explained Harstein. 'Their innards are moving around a bit, but there's not a lot of room in there. Ultimately that probably does contribute to a bit of fatigue at the end of the race and it's something that they feel, but it's all the mobile elements that are going to be submitted to significant G in what are basically four axes of movement, if we're not flying. There are some hills and so on, but the up-down is not that significant, generally. So they're being submitted to lateral Gs when they turn – Gs being a measure of how much acceleration or deceleration they're experiencing – and forward and backward Gs: forward G when they accelerate, backward or negative G when they brake. Newton's Law says a body in motion tends to stay in motion, so when the car changes direction, the head is going to want to stay where it is while the car is whipping around a corner. We can see on the television that there are some entries to fast corners which just look staggeringly violent, so you can imagine how hard the head is pushed to the outside.

'Those Gs can be quite significant. In the harder corners, they're probably pulling four or five lateral Gs – a big strain on the neck muscles, as obviously they can't just let their head go where it wants to go. They're really working to keep it steady, to keep their vision steady and maintain an axis. Same thing when they take off after a pit stop: their head goes back, they anticipate, they tighten their muscles. You can still see some pretty violent movements even when they're up-shifting, and also under braking. Their whole body's being pitched forwards into the belt, and their head goes forwards, so you're getting a lot of Gs being applied to this upper area and all these muscles are being severely put to the test. Controlling one of these vehicles is a fair amount of work. Now, the older guys are going to say, "It's not what it used to be", and they're right of course, but, nonetheless, I think that over race distance, over a day or a week of testing, they're really getting significant upper-body workouts.

'I said they're not subjected to a lot of vertical stuff. Obviously you have Eau Rouge and Liège, but they're not pulling a lot of vertical Gs. They are being subjected to tremendous vibrations however. When we go round in the medical car, which has good, reasonably stiff suspension, we see on the circuit where they're bottoming and we don't even feel it. When they're bottoming they've got a couple of millimetres of play. That sends this pressure wave right up their vertebral column, and doing that for 60 or 70 laps really is a big stress. I don't think their muscles can compensate for that – it's their vertebral discs that are doing that, their ligaments, their tendons. I think the long-term effects of that probably need to be looked at. Some of these guys when they're 50 are going to have the spinal X-rays of 70-year-olds. They're probably not going to get into immediate trouble with it because they're so young and healthy, and they'll continue to be healthy, but they're probably accelerating the wear and tear on their backs. Their knees get a bit knackered too because the cockpits are so narrow now. You'll see when they get out of the car that they're all wearing protection on the sides of their knees because they're banging on the sides of the cockpit, and there's some foam inside too.'

So, the cockpit of an F1 car is not a particularly friendly environment. It is cramped, noisy, full of strains and stresses, and very hot. 'Heat is a factor that kind of amplifies the other stuff,' Harstein continued. 'Since the 1980s they've known how to deal with heat. You see them drinking all the time. Noise is another big factor. They've got ear protection in, but the noise is being fed through the chassis into their heads, directly into the organ of hearing, and I think again it's something that just unconsciously contributes to this general level of information for the brain to process. When I say information, I'm not just referring to strategy, braking points, turning points, who's in front of them and so on; there's also noise, light, colour, all the information that's coming back from their various muscle groups that may or may not be useful. And, of course, the information coming from their arse, telling them "I'm getting into a little oversteer here", that is useful. Banging over the curves, that's not useful, but the brain's processing it anyway. So you have to realise that their brains are dealing with enormous amounts of information very rapidly. I think ultimately this is what makes these guys different from everybody else. People say that what makes F1 drivers so great is that they have hawk eyes and they have great reflexes. That's a bunch of bullshit. For me they are like fighter pilots, able to be at one with a machine and go incredibly fast in it while tracking targets and dealing with a computer that sets the missiles up. This is what makes all these guys so different: they're capable of dealing with enormous amounts of information at high speed. You hear Michael [Schumacher] on a qualifying lap on the radio … it's so hard to convey and to imagine.'

This, then – and it was an observation made by Sir Jackie Stewart and others in chapter 2 – is one of the key differentiators from the man in the pub, or the person sitting next to you at the dinner party. Drivers can process more information more quickly than others, and fitness is a great assistant in terms of enhancing what mother nature and inherited DNA has provided them. There is no doubt that physical fitness is a key factor in the make-up of successful motor racers. Ian Phillips bemoaned how so many pay drivers don't take this aspect of their lives very seriously. Maybe that is why they remain pay drivers. Just being there is good enough for them; the next step up requires a lot more hard work.

Joseph Leberer, a small, compact man from Innsbruck in Austria. knows all about hard work. He has been coach and trainer to many drivers. For years he worked with Ayrton Senna, now he looks after the drivers at BMW, Nick Heidfeld and Robert Kubica. I once shared a room with him in Suzuka during a Japanese Grand Prix when I was working for McLaren. He'd be up at five a.m., preparing breakfast for the Brazilian world champion. He travelled with seeds and nuts of all kinds, all 'biodynamic' he would assure me (these were the early days of organic food), which he would wash and soak so that they were soft and easily digestible by the time the great man got up. And if one of his charges had a pain, a crick, a pulled muscle, anything at all really, he would massage and treat the driver as often as was required, through the night if necessary.

Though you often see Leberer sprinting through the paddock clutching bottles of water and other paraphernalia for his drivers, fitness-wise he doesn't do very much for them over a race weekend. 'Over the weekend there's not so much any more because you have one race after another during the season. So it's more about recovering from the last race, relaxation and so on. We do active programmes to get the stress hormones out from their last race, some cardio training, stretching, running, cycling and swimming. Stretching the muscles helps to relax the body. During the race season they don't need a lot of specific training. They do a lot of tests, a lot of races, and we travel a lot and change climate, so you cannot do a fixed training plan, you have to adjust it. It's a question of whether the driver finishes the race and how many laps he gets through, and is there a test before the next race, and so on. I don't think it is necessary to do specific training for the neck or the body because racing so much conditions them anyway.

'The main work is done over the winter. November, December, January, February – this is the time when you do most of your training. You will start with a normal check-up, medical and physical, in terms of fitness, and, according to the results, you tailor your training and make a plan. If he's already a Formula One racer, and you know him, that will make things a lot easier. With a new driver, you really have to devise a completely different programme. Specifically, young drivers need to build up their core strength. This is very, very important. F3 is completely different to F1, where the loads on the body are quite enormous. It really is much more demanding. We have to work specifically on the core, and then on the whole body. The more you work in the off-season, the less problems you will get during the race season. This is something drivers need to understand, though every one is different of course. They have had a different upbringing, in different cultures. Some you can push hard as they are used to working hard. But the main thing is that you work hard in the off-season and then you can avoid injuries. It's very easy to get an injury if you overdo it, if you're tired and you overload the muscles.'

Leberer's experience is that most injuries occur in the upper body, especially the neck, lower back and shoulders, followed by chest and vertebrae. 'Some circuits have more bumps than others,' he observed. 'These can be a problem if you're tired, even dangerous, so, the fitter you are, the better. To be a top driver you need to be quite strong and have a high degree of coordination. Of course, as in most sports, the best thing is actually doing it – in this case driving. But it can happen that a new driver has to go straight into testing. Then you put him in a simulator and work on the muscle changes, building in lots of repetitions so that he gets memories to his muscles from the load. The point here is this: the better a driver can handle these loads, the better he can respond to the engineers. He won't have to worry too much about the physicality of driving an F1 car, and his talent can shine through. There is lots of information to process in a race car, so it's also better for his brain if he can rely on his fitness.

'A fitter driver is simply a better driver. Schumacher has set the standard for everybody. Some races are very hard and the climate can be very hostile; the air can get thin, things can be very demanding. It's always the fitter guys who will be in front. They work harder than the others, and it always pays off. For example, if a driver has the strength and focus to really push in the middle of a race – say he can turn out twenty qualifying laps – then he will be in front. And there is another aspect to this. If you're strong and you know how strong you are, you'll be more accepted by your team, and, if you are motivated, in turn you can motivate the team as well. You can expect the team to repay this by working brilliantly and indeed motivating the driver. In such an environment, strength breeds confidence. If a driver knows his limit, we can work hard, take him beyond these limits. The next step is he can challenge the other cars and be really competitive. Then it all starts to fit together. Then he's really racing.'

Food intake is crucial, and Leberer is very strict with his drivers in this respect. 'It's an important component of a driver's fitness plan,' he stated. 'This is their fuel. Some drivers understand this well. They are aware of their body and know diet contributes a significant percentage to being on top of their game. It's very important to balance the energy intake, so you get all the vitamins, all the energy you need for racing, but on the other side you shouldn't be so heavy, so full, that it takes too much energy to digest. We have to find a balance. Every driver is different. Drivers from different cultures use different foods, so you have to be aware of that and adapt. Again, it's good to practise diet options, to find the right routine, so on the race weekend you don't have to discuss things, you don't get an upset stomach, and you don't get tired. For example, Nick [Heidfeld] likes eating a lot, so sometimes I have to be careful that if there are good restaurants around he's not eating too late. My advice is to eat simple food, organically grown, as fresh as possible. The quality of the food is important. Race weekends can be tricky at times, and there is a danger of eating too late, and food that is not too easy to digest.' According to Leberer, these are 'small details which can really help'. Because of this belief he has always been very hands-on in this respect. 'I remember that, with Senna, Prost, Berger and Hakkinen, I did quite a lot of things for them,' he continued. 'I did all the cooking, for example, and brought a lot of stuff from home.

'In the end it does come down to a mixture of feelings for the driver, experience, and different therapies. Sometimes you really try different things, such as pressure points, complementary therapies and so on.' Leberer feels that, because drivers are required to use very specific muscles, and mostly in the same, repetitive way, it is important to train the opposite muscles, to help the body balance itself out and, indeed, prevent injury. And he has a novel way of getting some of the drivers to use these different muscle groups. 'If they have a two-week break from racing, as we do in August, it's best not to have them sit in the car and just do more of the same. Climbing, for instance, is perfect for stamina and strength, both mental and physical. You have to have a goal of where you want to go, and you have to know your next move. And if it takes two hours to do the climb, you have to learn how to conserve your energy. Again, knowing yourself quite well is a great positive in this context. It is about taking charge of things.

'If they really want to get to the top, they will do something on top of our training. They follow our instructions and our plans, but they try to do a little bit more. Of course you have to control them, but, in the end, the good ones will always do something extra, pushing themselves beyond the limits you have set them. Senna was incredibly strong in his mind, but he knew that to win you had to be good physically. Even if he was really in pain, he was so strong in his mind that he would finish the race. In the long term, if you want to be on top for years, you have to do the other things as well – that's what he did. You get stronger and stronger. But these days I would say that in general they do more. They know how important the physical preparation is.'

Over the years the Austrian has absorbed many lessons by being with these drivers, and has adapted his thinking in the light of how they reacted to his ministrations. It is, he said, certainly not a science, more of a feeling. 'I was lucky for years and years to learn a lot from all that went on around me. Drivers especially. They have to have talent, that is the first thing. Then it's hard work: all the skills, the willpower, the energy, the will to fight to go to the limit. Some of this you don't learn from your parents; you really have to learn it, work at it. And that is what we expect from these guys. And if they are too friendly, too nice, then these are not the people who can win a championship. They have to be smart, very hard, very demanding, be a leader. There is no room for compromise. I applied all this to what I do, as I learnt a little bit here, and a little bit there. When I was young I tried a lot of different techniques. As they worked, I gained in confidence. Again, just like a driver, you work it out yourself; you have to take your own responsibility. And it is very important for a driver to have a sense of how his body works, how far he can push it. Webber and Schumacher, they like to go to the limit, and this motivates you to do the same, to try different things, and your level of confidence rises too.'

Trainers and coaches like Leberer look at the season's calendar and plan their drivers' fitness schedules according to the pattern and sequence of the races. Some of these circuits are clearly much harder physically than others – the 'bumps' at the Belgian Grand Prix are a well-known example, as at Interlagos, where the cars also drive in the opposite direction and therefore the neck is loaded quite differently. 'The first ones are always hard,' Leberer revealed. 'For example, Malaysia is so hot. When we went there for the first time, we were amazed at how tough it was on the drivers. Only the guys who have worked hard the last couple of years can be on top of a circuit like that one. The pressure is huge, and it affects mainly the body's cooling system. Fitness in this case is really essential. The heat leads to so many things having to be done differently – to the car, but also to the helmet, to find better ways of cooling the head. This is a crucial area because, if the heat doesn't get out, it can become dangerous for the health of the driver. They can lose a lot of liquid, and this can lead to a drop in concentration. We also focus on their stamina, the capacity to endure. Also, reaction times are different if you lose a certain percentage of water and can't replace the minerals lost through sweating. So we are always looking to improve the cooling system inside the driver's helmet.

'Another tough race is Suzuka in Japan, as the corners are very quick. The Hungarian Grand Prix, held in August, is usually another tough race because it's normally very hot and there is a lot of gear changing, so drivers have little time to draw breath. Brazil's Interlagos in São Paulo has a very bumpy surface. The spine takes much of the brunt there, it will get very hot, and again it is hard for the drivers to relax as so many muscles are in tension throughout. Monaco is tough mentally more than physically. There is absolutely no room for error as there are no run-off areas. It requires total concentration at all times. Barcelona is also classed as a challenging race because it has long, fast corners, and therefore the drivers are subjected to prolonged high G-forces.'

When Leberer talks of 'relaxing' or 'having a break' during a race, it is all relative. It is not the language a normal person would use to describe the myriad activities still going on in the driver's cockpit, brain and body. This 'break' will happen in the straights, which some circuits have more of than others. 'Of course you're on full throttle anyway, but a driver can take time to breathe and relax the muscles for a second. This is also the time to take a drink.' Leberer feels that drivers who build these kinds of routines into their driving, knowing when and where on each racetrack they can take a deep breath, relax and maybe drink, are the ones who will do best.

We moved back to the subject of using other sports, like climbing, to train, which is something that is positively encouraged now, whereas not so long ago a number of the teams frowned upon their drivers engaging in so-called dangerous sports. Ironic, really, as their full-time sport is hardly danger-free. Nigel Mansell, despite the embarrassing short period with McLaren when he could not fit into the cockpit – which was really as much the team's fault as his own – was a naturally strong man, who loved to take part in the traditional Smudgers v. Snappers (writers v. photographers) football match that used to take place in Monza before the GP. One year he was a particularly fired-up and rumbustious centre forward. I remember it well as I was marking him. He was all elbows and hard body checks; he even sent one of the snappers to the circuit's medical centre because he was found to be passing blood after a particularly 'manly' challenge from Our Nige. Mansell loved it and, in return, the other players loved playing with him. During this particular match he managed to twist his ankle – not guilty, Your Honour – and after the match, in the early evening, he and I limped back to the semi-deserted paddock. At the Williams motor home Frank Williams and Patrick Head were chatting over cups of tea and were not best pleased to see their leading driver, on the evening before the race, limping along and telling them how much he'd enjoyed the match and how it was me who had tackled him unfairly, and so on. It was a lovely send-up of himself. Of course he exaggerated his injury, and the resulting expression on his team bosses' faces was unforgettable.

Leberer, of course, does not think F1 drivers should keep away from potentially dangerous sports. 'No, it's good for them,' he said. 'Of course rugby is dangerous, football also, but for me it's not a problem because, if you're in the car, it's a dangerous sport as well. The more you do, the better you are. Some drivers have it in their contract that they're not allowed to ski, for example, so each team takes a different view. But I'm a great fan of cross-country skiing: it's excellent for stamina, great for the back muscles, and very good for balance and coordination. To enhance focus and concentration, there's things like boxing or karate, again good for coordination and speed of reaction. There is decision-making too: when do I go, when do I hit, when do I have to be careful because it might hurt, how do I preserve my energy? These are good challenges and helpful, to some drivers, in developing better physical and mental attributes. Of course there has to be a top-notch assessment before embarking on this kind of training. We start with a full medical, then we go on to their neck and back, and we look at how they behave biomechanically.'

Looking at how drivers 'behave biomechanically' and tailoring individual training plans as a result is all a far cry from what went on in the days when Allan McNish started to drive cars, at the age of eleven. The Scotsman has had a full and varied career in the upper reaches of motor racing: he came through the lower formulae with Mika Hakkinen, he has test-driven in F1 for McLaren, Benetton, Renault and Toyota, he was a full F1 driver for Lola and Toyota, and he still managed to race sports cars, winning the Le Mans 24-Hour race in 1998 in a Porsche 911, and in DTM. Not the biggest of men, McNish's long relationship with fitness, and recovery from accidents, is a clear reminder of the progression in motor racing of the ever-increasing need for fitness.

'When I started racing, in 1987, drivers didn't have trainers,' he said. 'I'm not saying that it was the James Hunt era of Saturday-night parties and everything else. It was clean living, but not necessarily a real fitness requirement as it is today. That was partly because the cars didn't have the same level of G-forces. The first F1 car I drove was a McLaren-Honda, in Suzuka in 1990. That was, and is, a tough circuit, and a good lap then was 1:40. I went back in 2003, to fundamentally the same circuit, with the Renault and clocked 1:31.1 – nine seconds' difference. Nine seconds is a lot of G, and we were going down the straights at a similar speed, so it's the corner speed. From that point of view, we were 0.8 of a second quicker on every corner, and that's a significant amount of loading on the body. So there's a definite requirement now to train.

'Because we didn't have experts in the area of fitness, we did the usual things: we went running as fast as we could from A to B and we lifted as heavy weights as we could, but without any understanding of the best way to train, so it was totally inefficient. Then through the 90s there was a better understanding of how to do it, and also more of a requirement to do it. I would generally say that I train the same amount as I used to, but my efficiency is a hundred times better. And it depended on the kinds of cars I drove. In F1, you had to do a lot more work on your neck because of the lateral G-force combined with the weight of the car [600kg] – it was quite a load. On top of that you had to have a strong two-hour cardiovascular output, so it was high intensity, but for a relatively short period of time. But when I drove for Audi at Le Mans for example, we could be in the car for four hours. That is slightly less G load, but going on longer, the equivalent of two Grand Prix distances before we got out of the car. That is quite a difference in terms of the muscles required and also in terms of the type of training to get the longevity and endurance out of the muscle.'

McNish agrees with Leberer that the best way to train the body to drive a race car is to drive a race car. The lean frame of racing drivers has muscles in all the right places for what they have to do, especially considering the shape of the cockpit and that the position many of the drivers have to drive in is quite unnatural. 'After some years of driving your body – the backs of your shoulders, your neck, your heart and lungs – naturally builds up a resistance to the critical aspects of being a racing driver,' McNish told me. 'With F1 specifically, I worked a lot on the tops of the shoulders, because the steering wheel is higher than your shoulder line, so your leverage point is not as good. This is an area you have to work on a lot as it impacts greatly on your neck, because the position isn't perfect for the best neck angle to cope with the strong lateral G-forces. I also did a lot of fartlek running – for example, sprint for two minutes then come back to your normal jogging pace – or cycling uphill as fast as I could for two minutes, then bringing it down. All of this is designed to bring your heart rate up very quickly, then bring it down just as quickly. That short, intense kind of workout is very good. Now, with the Le Mans programme, instead of doing neck work with very heavy weights for a short time, I do slightly lighter weights for a longer period of time. I don't do as much fartlek, but I will do longer runs. So, for example, on the Tuesday night prior to the Le Mans race I will run round the circuit – so that's ten miles – with my team-mates. What I've discovered is that I don't need to drop my speed that much in order to run these ten miles. This must be partly because over a period of time your body does build up to this kind of fitness.'

McNish is convinced that fitness plays a crucial part in a driver's life and in his approach to racing, especially when the race is reaching the last third. 'When you come in for your final stop and put a new set of tyres on and go for it, you've got that strength to really attack. You also gain mentally as well because you know you're fresh and the other guy knows he's not, and he can still see you going for it and he can still see the gap increasing. Also it's very effective in testing, as we've got so many reduced days now that everyone wants to do as many laps as possible. In Barcelona I once did 147 laps in one day in an F1 car, the equivalent of two and a half race distances on a track with long corners and high G-forces. Normally you can only do one and a half hours before you start getting tired, so you've effectively got two hours of a test day when you don't utilise 100 per cent. That's seen from a team's point of view, but also from a driver's point of view, and again that comes back to a psychological thing. If you remember, back in Senna's day, he was quicker than the rest. The point was that he believed he was quicker than the rest, and the rest then agreed with him. In the same vein, he believed he was fitter than the rest. I remember seeing an interview where he was doing press-ups beside a pool in Brazil before the first race. You saw his main opposition lying beside the pool having a drink while he was actually working at it, and I'm sure that whole psychological effect helps.' Senna was also once famously pictured running bare chested during the winter break. He seemed to have a strap around his chest; in those early days of motor racing fitness, very few had any idea that this was a cardiovascular monitor. He was also the first of the drivers to train 'smart', going for shorter, more focused sessions.

Joseph Leberer was only one of the pioneers of this in F1, and McNish has had first-hand experience of working with him. 'I worked with Joseph in 1999 at McLaren, and it was an eye-opener for me as I hadn't done very efficient training until then. Joseph gave me the ground rules. Since then, sports science has evolved so much, but he was a real pioneer and understood things which others are getting into now. I have been racing cars for nineteen years. I get a sore back every now and again, and my muscles down the back on my right side are a little stiff sometimes from being on the throttle. I'm not necessarily in total peak condition purely because of the years of doing things in a cramped environment coping with high G-forces which your body is not naturally designed for. So now trainers are realising what Joseph worked out some time ago: that you have to counterbalance. You've got a muscle down the front of your body, you've also got a muscle down the back, and if you only train on one side, one of them is going to bulk up and the other one's not going to be strong enough to counterbalance it. I'll put it another way: if you carry a big briefcase on one side and not on the other, you dip down, whereas if you've got two, you're more balanced. It's the same with your body front to back as well. We're effectively doing a half crunch when we sit in the car. It's a very odd position: our feet are higher than our backside, our hands are higher than our shoulders, gripping on to the steering wheel. To counterbalance that effect we need to stretch the muscles out. This is where the idea of stretching comes from, like you do when you get up in the morning.

'What I've learnt in my years as a driver,' McNish continued, 'is that preventative medicine and preventative training are very important. Take the lower back, an area they've played around with in training but not really intensively. If you just think of the core muscles – that's been a real key phrase in the last few years, but it wasn't thirteen years ago. I know that when racing drivers get injured, which unfortunately does happen, the recovery period is much quicker because the muscles are holding the bones in place, particularly your spine. If you've got weak muscles, then the spine can move around, and if it can move in an accident, it's not got that same sort of strength to bounce back from it, so it can get injured more easily. This is why preventative training is a must. This includes stretching after training and after driving – something that again we didn't do a few years ago.'

To explain further the strains a racing driver is under, McNish told me that he was once strapped to a heart-rate monitor while driving in Monaco. Over a two-hour race, he averaged 168 heartbeats per minute. 'It's the equivalent of doing a run with your heart rate up for two hours. On top of that, you're turning a 2.5kg steering wheel; your neck is coping with 5G of load, which is like 40kg on your head instead of 8kg, and going sideways; and of course you're concentrating to your maximum, which is very tiring as well. And you're also twisting in the seat, lifting with your shoulders and running on the pedals. Then suddenly you stop. Now, what do you do after you have a really hard workout? You stretch. What do you do when you get out of a racing car when you've won? Pick up a bottle of champagne, spray it all over the place, have a drink, and that's it. So you will not get the time to stretch or relax properly.'

Again, McNish explained, there are areas where there are significant differences in terms of the stresses and loads for an F1 driver and a sportscar driver. 'For Le Mans you need to have some fat reserves, because you're basically burning a lot of energy for a long period of time and you can't just get it through carbohydrates and proteins, you need the fat as well. Now, I've got a very low fat content [i.e. body fat percentage]. It has been as low as 7.5 per cent; now I'm up to a heady 8.8 per cent!' For comparison, an average athlete might be 6 to 13 per cent, and an average fit male might be 14 to 17 per cent. 'I had to be very, very careful with rehydration because I didn't have the fat to absorb the fluids; also in making sure that I was always eating something, so I had bananas, yoghurts, soups, things I could eat quite quickly without having any real digestive time, because you can't sit down to a big meal because you could be in the car in an hour or something. Normally the ideal is pasta because it's a good balance between sugars and longer-releasing foods, but it makes me tired, I don't digest it. If I eat pasta I want to sleep, so I've found other ways to do it. Bananas for me are very good because I can eat them quickly and digest them just as quickly, and they're a good energy source. Fluid and food intake is critical, more so in endurance racing than in two-hour sprint races, whichever category it is, because endurance racers have to cope for longer with higher temperatures in the car.

'All racing in the heat is tough. Say it's 40 degrees centigrade. Whichever way you look at it, even if you lift your visor up to get some fresh air in, it's still coming in at 40 degrees. It's effectively like taking a hairdryer and blowing it in your face. We've got four layers of clothing on and we're in the car for over two hours. That's quite a hard physical situation. You can train, but, if you don't put the correct fuel source into your body, it doesn't matter. You are a high-performance engine, and you put the wrong fuel in it, forget it.' In order to combat the heat, experiments have been conducted involving special body coolers – as in the opposite of body warmers – but drivers find them clumsy to wear in the car. So many do what McNish does, which is to train in environments that mimic the conditions he will be experiencing on the racetrack. 'I'd go running, cycling at the worst possible time, the hottest time, or if it was a cold test I'd go early in the morning so my body gets used to the worst extremes that it's going to see. I think that's been a big benefit because I've also trained myself not to take fluids on board, because in the car they can and do fail. And that can mean fluid in a car with a lot of electronics – not advisable. So if I go running or cycling, I'll take a drinks bottle in case, but I'll try not to use it unless I have to. A lot of these things I do think are quite personal. Some drivers can't do that, some drivers really need the fluid, some drivers can't stand the heat, and that's their natural make-up. Even though I'm Scottish, I don't know why, but I seem to have a more efficient body at high temperatures than low temperatures. I think that's just a quirk.'

And, despite being Scottish, McNish insists that Leberer will never convince him to go rock climbing, as he is scared of heights. He also makes the point that good trainers will adapt to their drivers, because some will never climb, and others will have to be dragged kicking and screaming into the gym. 'Training only really works and is efficient when you enjoy it. If you hate going to the gym, you're not going to do it to the best of your ability, and you're also not going to want to go back as often. If you enjoy playing tennis that's much better than doing the equivalent in the gym. It's the Montoya thing. At Williams he was told he had to go to the gym. When he went to McLaren he had Gerry Convey as a trainer. He is one of the very best. He looked at Juan Pablo and knew he didn't like going to the gym, knew what he didn't want to do, and he created a training regime that was in line with how Juan Pablo would want to train, if he had to. I saw the result of this. While still at Williams he won in Brazil, but halfway through the race his neck had gone. Kimi Raikkonen was up his backside, pushing him, and you could see Kimi was solid on the neck for about another twenty laps. Brazil's hard on the neck because it's all left. One year later, now at McLaren, Montoya was the one solid on the neck and Kimi was the one with the wobbly head, and that was purely because he'd been developed in a different way. And that's not just about the driver, it's also about the trainer, about their understanding of what a driver requires. This is where I disagree slightly with the "it doesn't matter if you're afraid of heights" aspect. It's got to be what the person wants to participate in.'

Mark Webber, like Montoya, is no lover of the gym, but, unlike the Colombian, he looks super-fit and does much of his training outdoors. 'I'd rather be outside, or in the car, and testing is a good thing for the body because it's specific to the races,' he said. 'Also Frank [Williams] is good; he lets us do other sports. He understands you can't be wrapped up in cotton wool the whole time, that you have to enjoy yourself.' Webber is a particularly big fan of cycling and has been known to take time off to train in the US with a group of like-minded fitness fans, some of whom used to be involved with multiple Tour de France winner Lance Armstrong and his team. 'I love climbing, and I'm not a huge fan of riding on the flat, so it was good fun, and the sensation of going very high is good on the bike,' he remarked of one of these tours, in Colorado's Rocky Mountains. 'Though we didn't actually go up Pikes Peak [14,110 feet high] we went close. Some of the climbing was spectacular, the scenery phenomenal, with huge trees. The weather was nice, the roads were good, as was the company, and it was good training with those guys for a few days. So, a bit of riding and a bit of fitness testing – it was all good, and I had no problem adapting to the altitude as my stamina is all right.

'I generally enjoy fitness. It's not a chore for me. I enjoy testing myself and having a bit of fun with people who are like-minded, and obviously that spills over into my racing because it helps me in the car. Of course I'm very competitive when it comes to car racing, I love racing F1, so the way I do it is how I enjoy doing it. For example, the charity stuff I do at the end of the year, the Mark Webber Challenge, which is paddling, hiking and biking to raise money for kids with cancer, is also a good challenge. Being in good shape does help you in the car. Your condition makes you deal with the stresses that go on inside a car in an F1 race.

'People think I'm training like a psychopath every day, but I'm not, I just enjoy doing it. There's lots of drivers that are fit now, they're all training hard. But with back-to-back races, I don't do a lot in between. I just get ready for the next race. There's no one on the grid who's ultra fit. They're all fit racing drivers, but there's no one on the grid who's Superman.'

Johnny Herbert, winner of three Grands Prix with Benetton and Stewart in the 1990s, is another in the world of motor racing who is under no illusion about the importance of proper conditioning. The genial Briton is very popular with the media and, until he had his accident in F3000 in 1988, was considered one of the brightest prospects of his generation, once prompting Nigel Mansell, at Brands Hatch, to ask who was going so quickly in the Benetton test car. He survived the crash but nearly lost his legs, and though he went on to have a distinguished F1 career – there are still very few drivers who ever win a Grand Prix – he never managed to fulfil his exciting potential. Herbert, who was born in 1964, still drives now and looks very fit and much younger than his age. In 2005, in a somewhat strange career move, he was hired by Midland as a sporting relations manager in order to improve the team's public image in their final year as Jordan. His role appeared also to include mentoring, helping the new drivers settle into the unfamiliar surroundings of F1.

'Not really,' he countered. 'The guys we have here, they're experienced anyway, so they know what they need to do. In many respects they have to motivate themselves anyway, if they want to do this properly. They've got to get out there and work their pants off to get themselves into prime condition. There shouldn't be any panting when they get out of the car or anything like that, and, to be honest, I haven't heard any of that, so from that point of view they seem to be pretty much tuned up and in the right condition. The concentration in the races looks fine as well. So, at the moment, the preparation they've been doing has been A1. Last year [2005] was different, maybe. With Narain [Karthikeyan], the team always said he wasn't as fit as he should have been, but for me that wasn't the case. He'd worked hard enough on it, he just had a few other problems where he wasn't quite on the ball in terms of thinking about things and making decisions, but in the end I think he's grown up a lot. Obviously he's not here now, but Tiago Monteiro has got a lot better, and Christijan Albers is very much a fighter and always wants to do the best job he can – I think because of his days at DTM with Mercedes. That technique was probably impressed upon him very early on so he's just carried that through.'

Herbert was driving in F1 at the same time as Ayrton Senna, and, though he agrees that it was the Brazilian who set the new benchmarks for fitness, it wasn't like that from day one for the great champion driver. 'I know he came in after the first race, in 1984, and he was absolutely finished. That was where his training stepped up a lot. Obviously

Alain [Prost] was doing it anyway, but I think Ayrton upped it, and then Alain had someone to battle against. I think that just made that fitness level jump to another level. I think the way the cars were ... you had the big fat slicks on them, so the grip was very high anyway, you had the high G loads, and the wings were much bigger as well and the power steering wasn't there either, so you maybe had to physically have a little bit more muscle power. The fitness levels when I started had to be high because the only way you could do well was to basically drive the car hard anyway.

'Again, like anything, driving is the best thing: it always gives you the most, the extra technique or power you need in the car. But I think the process of [getting fit] has changed. The typical gym stuff you used to do, you had certain techniques; then five years down the line the newer generation of trainer comes along and says, "No, no, you can't do it that way, do it this way." They're always changing how fitness is done. It's now done more scientifically than it was done originally, back in the 1980s and early 1990s.'

Trainers, fitness plans, cross-training, medical check-ups ... I can just imagine James Hunt's quizzical look had he been confronted with any of these when he was driving. Of course, people have been training for their sport since organised events were first held in Olympia 2,700 years ago. And, though poor Hunt died at the age of 45, he was a natural athlete with the fitness to go with it. I recall one surreal moment when I was living in London and was cycling up St John's Hill in Battersea on my way back from the gym. I had a decent road-racing bike and was going at a fair lick. Suddenly I was startled by a booming, 'Hello, Norman. Put some effort into it, old boy. See you later.' Then Hunt passed me on a rusty, squeaky ladies' sit-up-and-beg bicycle complete with wicker basket over the handlebars and no gears. It was an unforgettable sight: longish blond hair streaming behind him, bare feet sticking out at 45 degrees on the pedals, long legs pounding away, a huge grin of delight on his face. Forget retirement and whatever problems he was having in his life at the time, I was ahead of him on the road and he had to beat me, he had to be first. And he was loving it. I can just imagine Joseph Leberer trying to adapt a special fitness programme for him ... though in the end Hunt would have gone for it simply because, if it helped him beat the next guy ahead of him, that was reason enough.

As Johnny Herbert mentioned, Alain Prost too was famously fit. He was also a cyclist, and each year he used to do one or two of the Tour de France's most gruelling Alpine climbs. Indeed he still does: in 2006, at the age of 51, he took part in a special Alpe d'Huez stage for amateur riders. Out of more than 7,500 participants he finished in 207th place, in 6 hours and 59 minutes. The top riders, all much, much younger than Prost, finished an hour quicker. This is an unspeakably tough étape of the Tour, and the amateurs follow the exact route of the pros. I did the route too, on my motorbike, and marvelled at every cyclist I saw. Hats off to Prost, fit beyond his years. It would have been nice, I thought as I motored along, to have seen Hunt and Prost battling up that mountain, then jockeying for position on the ultra-fast downhills. Now that would have been a race.

CHAPTER SEVEN

HE'S HAD A SHUNT

Pretty much no one in F1, indeed pretty much no one in motor racing, is keen to talk about accidents. There exists a series of euphemisms for what happens when a driver loses control of the car, or the car develops a problem, or a car and driver tangles with another. They speak of 'an off', or 'a shunt', or 'ending up in the kitty litter', for example. Racing accidents are part of a driver's life, and have been from their earliest karting days, and today's 'offs' are nothing like the carnage witnessed in the early years of F1, even as recently as the early to mid 1990s, but these innocuous, unthreatening, light-hearted phrases still describe one of the most terrifying experiences anyone could possibly have.

Like all dangerous sports, there is expectancy from the media and the public that something might go wrong. The extra frisson this gives is worth the price of the ticket and makes for good copy. No one wants anyone to get hurt, of course, but a big extra spectacle is always welcome. Sport insiders hate this of course, though they accept that the added excitement does put bums on seats, whether at home in front of the TV or at the event itself. Still, some of the accident compilations that come out on DVD, or are shown before the start of an event, are considered to be in bad taste by those who actually have to take part in the sport. I remember, when I was ski correspondent for the *Sunday Times*, being angrily upbraided by an Austrian coach because, on a visit to the UK, he had sat down to watch the BBC's *Ski Sunday* programme and been horrified to see that the intro sequence, with its upbeat music providing a surreal counterpoint, was mostly dedicated to downhill skiers losing their racing line and flying spectacularly into the air like rag dolls. Which at those speeds is exactly what they are. As I was the first Brit he came across when he was back at the races, he gave me a full, unexpurgated piece of his mind about the trivialisation of danger and how these people were very close to serious injury, even death, every time they left the starting hut, and how we were like voyeurs. And anyway, what did the British know about skiing?

It was a fun encounter, but I did fully agree with him. I was also covering F1 by then, and knew the human cost of having a shunt. Nothing can prepare you for witnessing an accident. Sitting in the media centre and watching it all unfold on TV is a surreal experience. First there is the collective shout from the several hundred journalists, then a flurry of questions: 'Did you see?,' 'Who was it?', 'Where did it happen?' When the replays start being screened it's fingers to the keyboard as the news agency and some of the daily newspaper journalists send their very first reports. Others rush out to the relevant team garage to try to get a first-hand feel for what is happening.

Having said that, the aftermath of an accident is often a very private affair with the media, thankfully, being kept away from the victim. Teams will close the garages if the accident appears to be bad. If the driver has jumped out of the car, then the media centre quiets down. And drivers will jump out of the cockpit and run back to the pits, if it's a testing or qualifying lap, hoping to get back into a car and continue. We see it time and time again. No sense of fear, danger or hurt; it is all washed under a wave of adrenalin. It seems incredible to those of us who are not motor racers, but it does seem to be part of the job description. But if the medical car lingers, if there is protracted activity around the cockpit, there is silence, as the media share in the worry for the well-being of the driver. F1, despite all the glitz and glamour, is a small world, and pretty much everyone knows one another.

Still, the role of the media can become very intrusive. My very first Grand Prix was at Imola in 1988, when Gerhard Berger's car went up in flames. At the time I was in the studios of RAI, the host broadcaster, quite by chance as I had gone to say hello to the sport editor; I was doing quite a lot of work for him in London, mostly on football. As we were chatting, the accident happened. He immediately went into 'war' mode, ordering the producers to get as close as possible, to carry on filming, to get better angles, to get closer, closer, closer. I was repelled and fascinated at the same time. It was the same with Roland Ratzenberger and Ayrton Senna. In the Brazilian's case the media intrusion was surreal. A number of Italian journalists had radio scanners and were listening to the off-air conversation between the producers and reporters.

Thus the press room knew very early on that poor Senna was dying as the off-air reports were relaying the grisly details of his head wound. I told my boss at the time, Ron Dennis, and he just gave me an uncomprehending look. It was not the right place, or time, to explain that some journalists were quite literally plugged into the Brazilian champion's last moments. Of course, anyone watching TV at the time would have seen Professor Sid Watkins, then in charge of all medical matters in F1, move away from Senna soon after he had arrived with the medical car. He knew his friend was beyond help, and his body language told the terrible tale.

My first 'live' accident, in the sense that I was not watching it on TV, was when Irishman Martin Donnelly crashed during practice for the Spanish Grand Prix at Jerez in 1990. I was behind the wire fence and I remember watching as the car disintegrated, and then seeing a hump, or a lump, on the asphalt. It was some way away and it took me a few seconds to realise it was Donnelly, still strapped into his seat, but with no other part of the car around him. He was just lying there on the circuit, not moving. A young woman got to him first. I can't recall whether she was a marshal or a paramedic, but I do remember she took one look at him, brought her hands to her face in horror, and screamed. Then she started waving frantically. Medical help came swiftly and Donnelly was then mercifully obscured from view. (Mercifully, too, he survived the accident, and drove again, in smaller club events. He also managed a Formula Vauxhall team. In 2004, he raced a Mazda RX-8 at a Silverstone 24hr race, and in 2006 he took part in a Lotus track day.)

I was reminded of all this many years later when I was on my way to the brand new Chinese Grand Prix in a van with some colleagues. About half a mile from the circuit we came across another van crushed against a tree, and another car half-wrecked and smoking. We instinctively jumped out to offer assistance, and that is when Donnelly's accident flashed back at me. I wondered what I would be able to do to help, whether I would scream too, whether I would be able to cope at all. Things worsened when we realised the van had been carrying the Williams marketing team to the circuit. People we knew. Some of them were lying or sitting on the road, others were still inside the van. There was quite a bit of blood about and, of course, much moaning. We did what we could to help, which was not much.

Before long a police car arrived, as did some rubbernecking local people, and, what with language issues and no crowd control, it was fast becoming a scene of chaos. Then another van arrived, and, as if in a movie, the door slid open and Professor Sid Watkins climbed out, followed by the entire FIA medical emergency team. They'd happened upon the scene by chance, but within seconds – literally – they had taken over, each one by an injured person, with the Prof, as he is affectionately known in the paddock, calmly standing slightly apart, assessing the scene and being fed quick reports by his staff. Had it been staged for the media, it would still have looked impressive. But this was for real, though luckily no one was badly injured.

The FIA medical team are definitely the people to have in your corner when anything goes wrong. As trauma specialists, they are used to seeing pretty upsetting sights, and of course they cope. But their job is made all the harder in F1 because they know so many of the people, the drivers in particular. Attending to an injured friend cannot be easy. The Prof has spoken and written poignantly about this, especially in relation to Ayrton Senna, a close personal friend of his. Improvements in safety have been spearheaded by the FIA, the sport's governing body, and Max Mosley. The Prof, though now retired from race involvement, is still active in the pursuit of increased safety, both in and around the car and around the circuits.

One of the most visible modern safety innovations is the strapping around the helmet called the HANS device. Gary Harstein, who has now taken over the Prof's role, explained to me how it works. 'The HANS provides an alternate mechanism for coupling the head to the body, other than the neck,' he began. 'In significant deceleration – whether forwards or lateral to some extent, mostly forward – the neck is subject to tremendous force because the head wants to keep going forwards and the body has been stopped by the belts. At some point the head gets constrained by the neck, and we don't want that to happen. So what the HANS does is provide an alternate coupling by attaching to the helmet and then down, so the helmet is attached to the HANS by some non-elastic straps, the straps are attached to the HANS, and the HANS is worn on the shoulders and held in place by a set of belts. So, in a deceleration, what now happens is the head moves forwards, tightens the straps, pulls on the HANS, and the HANS then levers because it's worn as a yoke over the shoulders; it levers forwards, clamps itself into the shoulders and stops the head from moving. So rather than it being the neck's physical mechanical limits, it's the fact that the head is coupled through the HANS to the shoulders that stops the head from moving. It significantly reduces the flexion on the cervical spine. You can imagine the head moving forwards; the cervical spine is flexed and pulled larger, longer, by that movement. Those forces are now very significantly reduced. It probably also has a significant effect on head injury itself, as the head is allowed to move a lot less. Since there's some degree of elasticity, the straps themselves give a little bit, but you can imagine that once the straps are tight, the HANS is going to gently – or not so gently – dig itself into the shoulders, and even that little bit of flexibility is going to cushion the deceleration on the head.'

Prof Watkins was asked many years ago by Mosley and Ecclestone to set up first-class medical facilities at each racetrack and to assemble a fast-reaction medical team that would be ready to go at a moment's notice. The sight of the friendly, white-haired neurosurgeon walking around the paddock in his blue race suit became a familiar one. During each practice and race session, the Prof would sit quietly in the passenger seat of a high-powered Mercedes, ready to be driven at speed to the site of any accident. Harstein has now assumed that vital role. 'What we want to check first [after an off] is that they're physically intact, and basically what that means to me is this. I'm concerned that in the event of another accident, they can egress their car rapidly without requiring help. They have an accident, they're not injured, the car catches fire … this happened a while back, with Michael [Schumacher] having to jump on his bad leg. Suppose he had an accident, the car catches fire, and his other leg is broken. Can he jump on his bad leg to get out of the car? We had him jump on it – absolutely brilliant. So what we're concerned with is not if they're in good enough shape to get on the podium – that's not my business – just, are they in good enough shape to get out of the car safely under their own power?

'Next, I want to make sure they are mentally OK, that their information-processing apparatus is up to it. In the past that used to be a bit catch-as-catch-can, a bit subjective. Remember, these guys are serious competitors, they're going to minimise all their symptoms. But for a couple of years now we've had a computer-based programme that objectively assesses neuro-cognitive function, and I've tested them all pre-season, so I have baseline data on them. Should they get a knock on the head, should I have any doubts about them, about their information processing, I'll run them through that test and that will objectively tell me whether they're back to where they were or they still need a little more time.'

That extra competitive edge which is a common thread running through all top drivers does make the medical team's assessment of the driver's condition crucial – hence the development and introduction of objective software. But there is still much wriggle room. 'The way it works officially is that I make a recommendation to the race director, who is the boss,' Harstein continued. 'I make a recommendation informing him that the competitor shouldn't take part in the rest of the event, and the race director will then take that under advisement, and usually carries it out. And there have been cases, such as Nick Heidfeld last year [2005] at Monza and Ralf Schumacher at Indy, where I didn't ban them from racing. I didn't tell Ralf he couldn't race, I told Ralf as a friend and as a doctor that he shouldn't race and I left a competent adult to make his own informed decision. Again, I can make recommendations, I can say "You need to go to a hospital", and, as a mentally competent adult, you can refuse treatment. If I feel very strongly about it and if they refuse treatment I have to report it to the race director, but that's never happened to me.

'So, realistically, what can happen is on four levels. Firstly, there's "Get yourself looked at and take a rest". Secondly, "We want X-rays taken, or we want this done, or we want you observed in a hospital". Then I might say, "I think you should take these" or "I don't think you should get in the car". I wouldn't use that informal level unless I was pretty confident that the driver could get in the car, but certainly I would never say it if I thought he would be in any way a danger to himself or anyone else. And then the last level is this: "You're not driving!"'

Harstein is an anaesthetist and an emergency physician, and he told me that the doctors at the circuits come from varied medical backgrounds, though all have significant experience in taking care of trauma patients. 'Often the initial approach to stabilising vital functions is the preserve of an anaesthetist,' he said. 'While surgeons are dealing with the ruptured liver, the ruptured spleen, the chest injury, the leg injury, which can be life-threatening, the initial approach is very often handled by an anaesthetist, and I think that's one of the reasons why Sid [Watkins] asked me to work with him. But, ultimately, there are doctors around the circuits of the world who have different backgrounds, [even] gynaecology and obstetrics, and I know some psychiatrists who have vast experience on circuits. The most important thing is to have trained and then to have had experience in handling injured patients.

'The first thing you try to do is avoid a secondary accident, so you need to stop in a safe position and make sure all the intervention crews are safe. The next question is how many victims are there, because the way you take care of multiple victims is not the same way you would take care of a single victim, because you have to spread your resources and therefore you have to prioritise. So that's a big question. Thank God, we haven't had to deal with that really, but it was a factor in 1998 when we had that huge incident in Spa where we could potentially have had twelve injured guys, though luckily nobody was hurt. The next questions focus on the driver: is he moving; is he out of the car; is he telling me he's OK? And those questions are by and large answered as you're approaching the car.

'Once you get close to the car you follow a fairly standardised approach. We use the pneumonic ABC. A is Airway – make sure there's an open, free and protected passage for air from the outside to the lungs. B is Breathing – make sure that the mechanism for breathing is intact, which means the brain is making the chest go in and out, and that the chest is mechanically functioning. And C is Circulation – you need to make sure that there is breathing, or if there's some other sort of shock state. If there is you need to stop to stabilise that, then prioritise the rest of it. You're thinking, "How am I going to get this guy out of the car? What are the dangers? Are things going to catch fire? Are there other cars nearby? What does the driver look like? How stable is he? How likely is he to be able to tolerate being taken gingerly and gently out of the car, or are things looking really bad and [will I] have to yank him out? Once you start going through this whole evaluation, and it can take some time, then you have to ask yourself: when do I want to get away from trackside and get to the medical centre? When Nick Heidfeld had his spectacular barrel roll [in 2005], I got on the radio and said to one of the pit-lane crews – generally we have three pit-lane crews of doctors – to go and evaluate him. Then he stopped at the medical centre and got evaluated. He was fine. We expected him to be fine, but these are competitors and they hate doctors as much as anybody else, so when it's like that we try to get them looked at. What makes my life much easier is that I'm dealing with extraordinarily fit young men who can take on board forces that the textbooks say can produce pretty significant injury.'

Crashes can look spectacular, and I wondered if Harstein has any way at all of anticipating what he will encounter when he races to an accident. 'Obviously when you see bits going everywhere, or if a car goes upside down, you think intuitively, "That looks bad",' he replied. 'My real answer is there is no absolute that makes me think there is no problem here, as anything can happen. You can have a severe injury from something bizarre happening, something that we haven't even thought of yet, so really all I want to see the driver do is take the wheel off and take off his belt. Even if he's in robot mode, severely concussed, that's better than being unconscious. What scares me is if they don't move for a while, though what usually happens is that they're actually on the radio saying, "Please don't punish me!" That always puts me a bit on edge. We like to see motion, we like to see thumbs up. I don't feel comfortable until I see him get out of the car, I really don't.'

There was, sadly, no 'motion' when Ayrton Senna failed to take the flat-out Tamburello left-hander at the 1994 San Marino Grand Prix and went on to hit a retaining wall at a sickening speed. I have heard it said many times that, had he not gone to Williams and stayed at McLaren, the accident would not have happened. I asked Jo Ramirez, who was very close to Senna, what he felt about that. 'For sure, I am one of those,' he stated. 'It doesn't take a rocket scientist to work out that the best driver in the world didn't make an error at Tamburello, which isn't a corner, it's a bent straight. Nobody ever lifted there, ever. So what happened? There was a concrete wall, and when [Gerhard] Berger had his accident, he had a couple of rolls in the same place. He badly damaged the car and whatever, but he was OK. This particular year they didn't have a single row of tyres there. Well, it's straight; nobody's ever going to go off there. But if you do have a problem, then you go off right there, and there is a little bump there. Now, if you hit that bump, at that speed you take off, and Senna was in the air quite a long time. When he touched the ground he hadn't lost any speed, because he was in the air, so when he touched down he was too close to the wall and he hit it at incredible speed.'

'He jumped up because of that little bump?' I asked.

'Yes,' Ramirez replied. 'He couldn't get the corner . . .'

'... because of the steering,' I finished for him.

There was silence between us. We were both at the circuit at the time, but I knew Ramirez would know much more than me, and it is still a very touchy subject for many people in the sport. I suppose it's like the silences that reign in the climbing community after a tragedy. Ropes get cut, people go down, others are saved. Hard to explain to outsiders. Life must go on.

'I could say so much about it,' Ramirez continued after a short while, 'yet sometimes I think it's better if you don't say it. It's been over ten years. And, because it all happened in Italy, it made things more complicated: it seems that there you cannot have an accident, somebody has to be responsible for it. So they tried to dig and dig. Senna and Prost always said the cockpit on the Williams was horrendous. They had to have a smaller steering wheel, and Ayrton hated it; he just didn't want it. It was too low, they couldn't move their legs, and, when Prost complained bitterly, the response was, "This is the car, you drive it." Prost told me, "I remember at McLaren, I had maybe five or six [seat] fittings until I was happy, and if I wanted one more they would make one more, until I was happy. After that they never had to make another seat. But at Williams we had one, I didn't like it, and that was it. I just had to adjust. They wouldn't do another one." But Senna being Senna, he turned around and told them, "Have you tried the car? You cannot drive it like that, you have to move the steering wheel." I'm not blaming Williams: they wanted to do it; they tried to accommodate him in the car by doing this modification. It was silly how the court case went on for so long, as if Williams wanted to kill the best driver in the world, who they were paying $50 million a year. He wasn't at fault, and Williams wasn't at fault either.

'The Williams just wasn't a good enough car for them to win races. Michael Schumacher knew the car was bottoming out and he said there was no way he could have driven the whole race like that; he would have had to slow down because he wouldn't have been able to keep up that speed. In the end, it was one of those stupid things; one row of tyres there would have saved Senna. What killed him was that the wheel came off, the suspension came off, and if he'd just hit it an inch further up … It was horrendous. It's one of those things that you just never expect to happen. I remember we used to have the big table in the motor home and all the engineers would go on working late at night, and we would talk. On the Friday we had the Rubens Barrichello accident, then on Saturday it was Roland Ratzenberger. That Saturday I remember saying that it was the poor guy's first race; he was practically unknown. A couple of weeks in, people forget, nothing is going to change. We hadn't had a fatal accident for twelve years. Elio de Angelis was gone, and now Ratzenberger. "Imagine something happening to Ayrton," I said. He was one of those guys who'd been in for long enough; you just think it's not possible that anything can happen to them. I was certain it would never happen. For sure I wondered if he'd stayed at McLaren ... I remember that's what the family told me too. But for sure, I said to them, nobody tried harder than me to keep him at McLaren, and we all did in our different ways. Ron was really trying to get the money to do it again, because he was worth it.'

I wondered why and how Dennis let Senna go. It seemed out of character. 'Mainly because we lost the Honda engine,' Ramirez said. 'We didn't have an engine manufacturer. Ron thought that maybe we would have had the Peugeot, which in the end didn't work. But at least if we'd had a big manufacturer coming in it maybe would have convinced Senna to stay. You just never know.'

CHAPTER EIGHT

ANDY PRIAULX

A ndy Priaulx has already briefly appeared in this book, in chapter 3, but it's worth devoting more space to him for two reasons. First, in some ways he is easier to understand as a driver. He wears his fears, ambitions and successes on his sleeve and is more willing to share than some of the more rarefied F1 drivers, many of whom have lost the ability to relate to ordinary life situations. Andy is not on megabucks, yet he drives in a very competitive series, the World Touring Car Championship, and here comes the second reason: he has won it three times, consecutively. The clinching and last race in 2006 was in Macau, a fiendishly difficult street circuit that allows no margin for error. There are no run-off areas and at all times the cars form a very tightly packed group. Priaulx says he is the most successful British racing driver, and he is. Those world titles tell the story. So here is what he thinks being a racing driver is all about.

'Some drivers can just rely on their natural ability and they do all their work in the cockpit,' he began. 'There are other drivers who have to do a lot of the work out of the cockpit. The drivers who naturally do it in the cockpit and succeed are great drivers; the ones who do it out of the car then get in the car and succeed are also great drivers. But the ones who can actually do it in the car, naturally, and then apply themselves out of the car as well – like Schumacher, for instance – are exceptional.

'When I started out it was very tough for me. I had great results in the lower championships, as I was a natural driver. But then it became very, very difficult. Funding is a big issue in motor racing. There are a lot of things out of your control, though you do your best to try, and that takes a lot of energy from you. That causes your performances to drop away because it adds a lot of pressure on top of what is there already. For example, you might have managed to get £20,000 out of a sponsor for one race. Of course they want to come and see you win. But you don't, because you haven't sat in the car before, and they wonder why you're driving round in tenth place. That's pressure. Then you start trying to drive harder, and, of course, you start to overdrive. I had a very difficult time when I won the British Hillclimb Championship in 1995. I was really blown up as a driver, and then I went from hillclimbing into circuit racing, which is a bit like being a top tennis player and being given a table tennis bat, and you're expected to win the next day. I didn't win. I still had good car control, but I was miles off winning, and I really needed to understand how the whole thing ticked. I spent two or three years struggling. Maybe I was talking too much and not performing, trying to overcompensate.'

This is the period in his career when Priaulx discovered how meditation could help. The result? World titles 'with the smallest team in the pit lane, and still with big monetary challenges. I'm not paying for my drive any more, but you're suddenly dealing with a manufacturer who might want something else and you've still got the same issues. But I'm able to keep that away and still perform, and I've got some interesting techniques to allow me to do that, and that's why I use the meditation. A lot of drivers just purely rely on natural ability, which can only get you so far in motor racing.

'I think you need to be your own worst critic, but in a positive way. Instead of running yourself down with criticism, turn it into a positive and say, "Well, I can improve in these areas, and then I can go to the next level." Tiger Woods writes a checklist of things he needs to do to improve his swing. I do a checklist at every race weekend of all the positives I need to have on my side: good diet, good sleep, the right vitamins, all the positives I need from the team, make sure this is right and that's right with the car, and everything else. So you've done your work before you get in the car. I'll also have done my research on the circuit. I'll look at the circuit and imagine all the different scenarios – dry, wet, damp. What will I do if they try to overtake me here? So I've done my preparation. You have to be able to deal with things if they do go a little bit wrong, and that's where I think my working method allows me to think, "OK, the car's not quite right so I'll bury myself in the car, understanding myself, my data, my performance, the team, everything around me, and pushing everything outside that away. Then I'll be able to attract a good result." Yes, you're making your luck. If you're in a car that's capable of tenth place and you finish eleventh, you've let yourself down. But if you finish tenth, you can walk away feeling that you've achieved the best you could with the tools you had that weekend.

'Being able to do that, week in, week out, that's very difficult. I do believe that there's something special with sportspeople who can do that. I believe in looking for people's auras. You can feel an aura. If Schumacher walked in here now, you'd know about it without even looking, because he's got an aura. I had to develop mine, some have one naturally. Senna, when he was in Formula Ford, people were looking at him then. There's something very spiritual about very successful people like him. Mansell's story's a bit more like mine. He had to go and clean windows to make it happen. But he still made it happen and he still won the Formula One World Championship. My career started a bit late. If I had started earlier and hadn't had such big monetary challenges like I did, I could have gone further. When Mansell was driving it was a little bit different: in those days you could get a Formula Three drive funded by Unipart or whoever, whereas now it all relies massively on the driver. Even in F1 it is up to the driver to find the money very often, and that was very difficult for me to deal with. But I do believe that there are very special sports people who have that natural aura which attracts people to them, and they don't have to say anything. It's quite spooky actually. It can make the hairs stand up on the back of your neck. You can't put your finger on it, but they've got something different.

'Mine wasn't a massive belief in myself, more of a massive desire channelled in the right way. If you truly want something, then the whole universe helps you. It's like an underlying current that pushes you in that direction. You always go in the direction of your most dominant thoughts, whether that's failure or success. At a particular race I might have 70kg of weight, so I might not get a win. But I focus my thoughts on that end result, which is winning the championship at the end of the year. I've got to make sure in my mind that I've covered all the possible eventualities, and, if I've dealt with them in a positive way, I'll still be happy with or without the title because there'll still be things I've achieved during the year which I'll be very happy with. It's all about keeping yourself at a high level of positiveness, keeping that energy flowing in the right direction.

'In Macau in 2005, the last race, there were three drivers capable of winning and there was a lot of interest in me [as reigning champion]. In 2006 it was the same, except that nine people were in the frame. Both times I just imagined a positive energy coming in. Look at Mansell in his years of racing when he'd try to go round the outside of someone – he was using the positive energy of his fans to drive better. Schumacher did it too, and Alonso's got it now with the Spanish crowd. You've got to be able to turn things round and you've got to be able to see that energy and take it. You just have to stay positive because if you're looking in the rearview mirror when you're driving forwards, you will crash. It's also about being able to take a positive from a day that's not been so good. You have to have the determination within yourself to be able to look at a bad weekend, understand why it's bad, take that understanding to the next weekend and turn it into a positive. That's very hard.'

I told Andy that I once asked Michael Schumacher about meditation. He said he'd tried it, but it wasn't for him. 'He closes his eyes on the grid,' Andy countered, 'and that's a form of meditation. He does do it, but he'll do it naturally. It might confuse him and maybe he doesn't need it, but there are people who need their thoughts channelled. I'm very into line maps and things like that, ways of understanding the big clutter of information and changing that information so you can memorise it. A lot of people don't use their memory; they don't use their mind enough.

'In World Touring Cars you've got manufacturers paying the bills, but they still don't like spending money. Whether it's a sponsor or manufacturer, they don't want to pay millions of pounds for crash damage, because that can go towards developing the car and making it faster. At the same time, all the testing you're doing, you've got to be able to use that mileage and put it into the development of the car. Each lap and every lap is crucial. People just don't realise how much energy and concentration go into every lap. That information, and each lap, can take you closer to your goal. I always said I'll make every lap count over my career. On a test day, when I do 140 laps, I make every lap count. The concentration has to be very high. You mustn't manhandle the car but drive it with sensitivity, to understand mentally what's happening, and be able to translate all this into quality feedback for the team, information they can understand. And to be able to do that all day and for your last lap of the day to be as good as your first, that's the difference. When I look at drivers who stand on the pit wall and spend a lot of time standing round, those guys could be working. This is the difference with a Schumacher: he'll be in there understanding every bit of data, he'll do a lot of the testing himself, he understands what's going on, and he can manipulate and move things forwards in his direction.

'You have to learn to find your talent. A lot of drivers don't apply themselves. You see a lot of drivers with wasted talent – they haven't applied themselves. At the same time, you see sportspeople who have just been natural. But I believe that nowadays you have to be natural, especially in F1, and have massive application. When Alonso won his first world title, he was the first on the plane home the next morning. He wasn't out partying all night, he was very serious about it. Maybe that's not great for the sport in terms of celebrity value, but at the same time he is world champion. There's something that makes those guys, Schumacher and Alonso, tick. I bet they've both got that mental attitude, whether it's natural or whether it's been trained. A lot of decisions in F1 you can't influence directly, but maybe indirectly, without realising, your subconscious can.'

Talking of learning to find your talent through application, Andy revealed that his biggest problem when facing the challenge of getting his driving back on track was that the process might take him away from his natural driving. 'I started to think about my driving like this: brake here, the data says brake here, lift off, turn in, get on the power. I was thinking about all the wrong things, whereas I should have been thinking about how I could prepare myself and the team so that when I got into the car and drove it, it was my natural driving. I always remember the time when I first jumped into a go-kart. Nobody told me about understeer or oversteer, I just did it. My son's the same. He's five years old, but you put him on a little buggy and it slides, he'll counteract it with oversteer. Nobody's told him about that. That's what you've got to attract, that young boy within yourself who does things naturally, and put it with the old experienced head that knows what's happening. Senna talked a lot about this. He would have been more into meditation and things like that than Michael. Senna was religious. And a prayer is meditation.

'To begin with I had somebody I worked with – a mentor, a driver coach – but then, as I said, I developed my own special simple techniques. For instance, I managed to train my mind to the point that when I pushed the starter button on the car I recalled times when I'd driven really well. I recalled how I was feeling and all the things that went right that day. I can key into that zone in a snap of the fingers when I press that starter button. I imagine my body as connected to the wheels, to the throttle, to the steering, to the rear wheels, to the brakes – I just imagine the whole car as an extension of my body. I know you've heard all this before, but I do, literally, feel that in my car. I've actually almost got to the point where I have an out-of-body experience in the car, and on those days there's no way you're going to go off and make a mistake. It's very similar to when you're playing football and you're looking at the goalkeeper and there's no way you're going to miss the goal. You're going to thump it in because you're keyed into the zone. Or you're running down the right wing, you're just about to chip the ball in, but instead you lay that ball off right in front of the centre-forward, and he pops it in the goal. It's that sort of driving: you know exactly where the car's going to end up, and you're absolutely keyed into where the brake points are and what's going on. There are no extra corrections with the steering, there are no nasty down changes. It's so natural, so special. That is the buzz of driving when you're in that situation. You're driving the tyre to its level of grip and not beyond. Now I can understand ten grams of pressure, I can feel it in the tyre. The team is making an adjustment to the tyre pressure, it's minor, but I'm feeling it. It's that level that's so important in a race car, to be able to feel or communicate that sort of information. You've also got time to think about other things because you're not thinking about your driving. Your capacity is being used in other areas; you're relying on your natural intuitive driving.

'It's almost like the door was ajar and you just pushed it open and there was a whole new world, a different level of driving. It's like Senna used to say: you go to a level and you find a whole new level, and you get to that level and you find a whole new level. As I've got older I've begun to appreciate that more and more. I'm actually understanding where those levels are, whereas, when I was younger, I perhaps went beyond, crashed, and learnt from my mistakes. And you've got to keep going. I'm always adapting as I believe you've got to change. I've got a nice saying: "If you stand still, it's like going backwards at a hundred miles an hour." I look at the weekends when I've driven really well and try to improve on that. For example, Macau in 2004, where I put the car on pole with 62kg of success ballast, with all the pressure of the championship on my shoulders, having raced all year, and it was down to the last race and there were walls everywhere. I managed to take my driving to another level that day, and now that's the level I hope I can continue from.

'The only annoying thing with motor racing is that there are a lot of things that can influence your performance that are out of your control. But you've got to appreciate that, and understand that it's like destiny – you can't change it. You can actually blame yourself for it though. I recently raced at the Nürburgring in the 24-hour race and I actually said that, if I had a crash, whether it was with somebody or not, it would be my fault. It's one of those races where most of the time you do get involved in somebody else's accident. Funnily enough I went all weekend without crashing. It was like in football again, almost having that awareness of where the striker is and without looking you just place the ball there. You can almost set up an aura around the car. People used to say that when they saw Senna's yellow helmet in the rearview mirror, they would get out of the way. That's an aura working.

'I'm sure if you put the top ten drivers in the same F1 car on the same day with the same tyres and the same fuel load, they'd all be within a tenth of a second of one another. But it's the guy who can do that week in, week out, with or without a bad car, on every different circuit, whether he feels good or not, and take things to another level – that's the difference between a champion and a good driver. And that's how I do it, so I am changing all the time. On the other hand, I do like to eat the same foods, and I like to have an "hour of power" before I get into the car where I'm geeing myself up: I have a little sleep, and when I come round from my little rest I'm at that nice level where I'm relaxed. The times I've woken up from a sleep, usually in the middle of the night, with a solution to a problem with the car ... it's unbelievable. You're just about to go to sleep, you're just relaxed and chipping away at it, and you find something. It's quite spooky. There are quite a few techniques for this, like the glass of water trick, where you drink a glass of water while you're thinking of a problem and then you imagine that's the problem going into you and you deal with it and then you wake up in the morning with a solution.

'I believe it's all about tuning in to the right brainwave frequency. Usually we're at beta frequency, where it's all about smell, touch, taste. You can go to a deeper brainwave frequency, the alpha level, which is more like dreaming, and that's where you're at your most intuitive. If you can bring your driving to that point ... That's what Michael Schumacher does on the grid when he closes his eyes. He's going down to alpha. When you're young your brain works at alpha and that's why you can take more information in. Your memory's better when you're five, six, seven, eight years old. But as you get older your frequency goes up and up; you take in less and you remember less. The alpha level is where I believe you need to be in the car to drive really well. Then you're able to memorise the car, what it's feeling, what's happening, when to pit, when to overtake. It's almost like you can feel someone's about to overtake you before they've even done the move, and you're there for it. That's the alpha level. That's what you need to be able to attract.

'Often in the car I try to defocus my eyes so that I'm not concentrating on any one thing. I'm taking everything in with peripheral vision, yet I'm driving beautifully, taking in every inch of the road. I'm not looking at the car or at the apex point, I've got a general understanding of what's going on. I'm just able to take the ideal line, able to drift the car over, using half the white line on the exit with a little puff of dust – perfect placement of the car. It's all about finding those times when you've driven really well – when you haven't thought about it, when it just happened – recalling them and using them again and again. You're not asleep, you're just at that level where you've got 100 per cent aggression with 100 per cent restraint. You're hitting the nail on the head every time, never missing, week in, week out. Schumacher and Alonso, I believe, do that. They've got their own natural way of doing that.

'Formula One hasn't necessarily got the best drivers in the world, but I do believe most of them deserve to be there because they've attracted it in some way. I also believe they've all got stuff to learn. They all need a mentor, a driver coach. I know that David Coulthard has looked into this a bit, and DC's performances have improved. I believe that there's a long way to go with that side of things as well. Just having somebody, a driver, looking at your data, and translating that information into something where you can then speak to the driver involved and give him a natural feeling of what he should be trying to achieve. You can look at a line on a sheet of paper and you can convert that into a feeling, and that's what we do. You say you need to go a bit later on the brakes, and we're converting that into how it would feel that much later on the brakes. How will the car feel when we go out a bit faster? What would I need to do if we went later on the brakes? Would I need to look further ahead? Would I need to anticipate the corner more? Would I turn earlier, or slightly later? The engineers don't know that. They're looking at a line and saying that's what the line does and this is what you need to do, but they don't tell you how to do it or how it might feel. At the end of the day, driving a car is all about feeling. You've got the data to give you an idea of where you're losing it, but you've got to translate that data into a feeling, and that's what's difficult. When they reach that barrier a lot of natural drivers don't know how to overcome it, and that's when a guy who's worked at it and who does know can help. I've heard Gerhard Berger say that very often the working driver can get to a higher level than the natural driver because he works at it, he understands it.

'For instance, when you put on a new set of tyres, you need to improve your anticipation. The car's going to be arriving a little bit faster so you've got to extend your vision a bit further, you've got to look to the exit a bit sooner. I've actually experimented with people in the car, people who've had no driving experience at all. I've just got them to look further ahead, and it's made them faster without even trying. It's like when you play squash. You've got to look at the ball, you must never take your eye off the ball. You're running around, but you're never taking your eye off the ball. As soon as you take your eye off the ball you've lost it. And you've even got to watch the ball almost come off the racket.

'So, it's about natural ability: your speed, eyesight reflex and coordination are such that you probably can almost see the ball coming off the racket. But most people, even relatively fit people of our age, won't see that.

'There's a lot in reflexes, and I've had my trainer throwing balls at me from behind and I've been catching them. You do need that, but it's also about training the peripheral vision – you need some of that too. I've done the whole personal trainer thing. I'm very motivated with my training, but very often people like that can be a distraction because they want you to go and ride a bike on a Friday afternoon when you should be thinking about qualifying the car and it's not going to make a difference. Mansell is a prime example: he wasn't ultra fit, but he still found a way of getting through the Grand Prix and winning it, even if he did collapse on the podium and it was all a bit of a drama. He still found a way to win the championship. It's all about having priorities really. He was a naturally strong person, a bit of a Montoya really. When you see him, he's got a bit of a paunch on him, but he's strong. He'll hang on to a motocross bike on a flat-out section over bumps and he'll be all right, whereas Michael [Schumacher] probably does need to do the training because he's quite a small-framed person.'

At this point I told Andy that I recalled walking behind Fernando Alonso at the airport in Australia and realising that the Spaniard was built like a welterweight boxer. He even held his shoulders slightly forwards. Big head, big neck, not particularly broad in frame, but strong. He has a distinctive V-shape. 'Compact and efficient,' Andy summed up. 'I think we are all going to talk a lot about Alonso in the future, and though I don't know so much about Raikkonen, I think he's a natural driver too.' I ventured that he also seems to have a self-destruct button. 'I think motor sport needs a bit of that as well,' Andy said, 'because it's exciting. Otherwise you'd be bored shitless basically. And you need all kinds in this sport. I love looking at DC now because when you saw him in his McLaren days he was one person. Now you see him in his Red Bull Racing period and he really is quite different. You can see he's really got his head screwed on. I'm sure that when he finishes his career he'll get a lot of offers to run teams because he's got that whole experience thing. Like [Gerhard] Berger, people like that – they've just got it. But something's missing, isn't it, with DC? Just something you can't put your finger on. He might be getting to the point where he's had enough. I really would love to have seen him in a more competitive car. I know he nearly won the championship, but he was up against a lot at McLaren.

'I know teams like that wild streak, like the Raikkonen streak,' Andy continued, returning to the subject I'd introduced. 'Drivers like that have natural speed. Teams like them. They like the challenge because they know those drivers are good. But the key point is whether they can actually get them to apply themselves. I've had team-mates who've been naturally good drivers but, as soon as they've tried to apply themselves, they've failed. Some drivers can't do it. And some drivers are not comfortable in their teams. Everything's very well organised, everything's there, but it's not supportive. Raikkonen likes the odd drink now and again, and likes to play ice hockey – Ron [Dennis] would have no sympathy at all with that. I suppose someone like [Flavio] Briatore might have been more understanding. If a guy wants to go and play ice hockey, ride motorbikes, he'd say OK, let him do it. Otherwise it destroys the relationship, and his attitude to the team becomes negative. That's where you need a performance consultant to stand between the team and the driver, and I can see that so many times with teams. When I finish my career, I'll offer my services to a team and a driver and stand in the middle and see if it will work.'

I asked him about fear, telling him that many of the people I'd spoken to said they had none. 'It's bollocks, all day long,' Andy came back. 'I believe you need to have fear to be quick. I was the most nervous driver ever, each time I sat in the car, but I've overcome it. I believe you need that fear so you can turn it into a positive. Then you become really fast. You don't want that thought of fear when you're in the car and when you're driving; it'd be blocking you. You just have it when you get into the car and then you overcome it. You have to identify fear and face it. It's only the inner voice trying to tell you you can't, and you're saying you can. If you can overcome that then you've won. I call it my "monkey mind". It's always chattering away at me, preying on my fears. Senna overcame this, and Michael's got a dismissive way of blocking it out. But everybody has fear, and being fast isn't about being brave, it's about being confident about what you can do in the car, and being committed to the risk. When you're not committed to the risk you're at your most dangerous – a little bit hesitant. If you're in a committed frame of mind and you say, "I'm going to go in, I'm going to turn in with that commitment, and I'm going to put the car there", you will. If you're not committed to the risk you will have a crash.

'You really do need to know how to overcome the monkey mind. It's the last 2 per cent, the crucial bit. You overcome those sorts of things in testing all the time. You just hone your skills and before you know it – you don't even realise it – you're at a high level, you're driving in that band and you have no fear at all. There is total confidence and belief, and, even when you go off, it's not because you made a mistake. You know you can go through the next lap at the same speed. I had a couple of instances last year where I had a big accident. A tyre blew and I went straight into the tyre wall at 140 miles an hour. They fixed the car and I went through the next lap at full speed. Not bravery, just total confidence. I don't believe I'm a particularly brave person; it's just that I've honed my belief, I've controlled the monkey mind, I've worked with it, I've got that feeling, that intuition, that understanding. I know what I can achieve and I know how to achieve it. That's just confidence.

'Stirling Moss once told me about [Juan Manuel] Fangio at Monaco. In those days [after an accident] they weren't so quick: the marshals would first run to the car, then they'd go back and get their yellow flags. Fangio used to watch the crowd to see where they were looking during his lap. That's clever, and that's how you stay alive in motor sport. That's the same mentality as Jackie Stewart. And that comes purely out of fear, nothing else. Fangio was shit-scared but he was still able to win five titles. People died, and he was scared. And how do you get in a racing car and commit yourself in that way? It's just confidence, that's all it is. Belief in your ability, and understanding.

'I think the biggest fear, more than the fear of having an accident, is the fear of not doing well. When I lined up for my last race in 2005, all I wanted was to leave no doubt in anyone's mind who was the best driver that year. I'd won the most races, and, whether I deserved to win the championship or not, I just wanted to leave no doubt in anyone's mind about who was the quickest. It felt like the whole of the universe was pushing me to do well. There were three guys who could win it on the day, and we were all separated by one point. The others hit the self-destruct button, but I was just able to press the starter button, attract the good feelings, let other things bounce off me, and get into the zone, and it brought the championship. I attracted the championship. It's mental at that level, that last bit. It's so much about belief.'

In November 2006, after two races absolutely to the limit, the last ones of the season, Andy Priaulx won his third title. 'Standing on the podium as world champion was special,' he said at the time. 'Last year was easier as there were only three of us fighting for the title and I more or less had it sewn up in race one. This year there were nine of us. I don't reckon if I had been in F1 the pressure could have been greater. Before I finish and hit the party, I also want to say a big thank you to my own personal Buddha. I bought him here in Macau last year, he guided me through to the title then, and he has done it again this year. I don't wear him because I am superstitious or anything like that; it is more a feeling of comfort while he is round my neck and I am in my BMW racing car.'

CHAPTER NINE

TEAM BOSS

Team bosses in F1 are as different from one another as the colours of their cars. They are of different nationalities, of course, but they also fulfil different roles, depending on the team, who owns what, which engine deal they have, and who is the primary sponsor.

Things were a little bit simpler up until the early 1980s. In those days they were called 'constructors', because that is what they did: they built cars, slotted in an engine (usually a Ford Cosworth), and went racing. Many of the teams were, and some still are, named after the original constructor: Ferrari, obviously, but also McLaren, Williams, Tyrrell, Ligier, Minardi, Jordan, Brabham, and so on. So the team boss was exactly that: lord and master of all around, from the factory to the car to the driver. It was a precarious existence, and the advent of big-name sponsors was a natural development in a sport that was beginning to require deep pockets and staying power. Marlboro and other tobacco companies took a lead and brought money and new thinking into the sport. The appointment of Ron Dennis as the new leader of McLaren was one of the more significant of the big commercial deals put together by the sponsors, who began to have much more of a say in the way teams were run, and in which drivers were taken on. The next phase saw wholesale takeovers, such as the Italian textile company Benetton taking over the Toleman team (in 1985) and installing a professional manager, Flavio Briatore, from outside F1 to run it. Then engine manufacturers started to take a much more active role in the way the teams were run, often clashing with the original constructors: Mercedes and BMW are examples of this, as they moved into (or at least tried to) McLaren and Williams. The final phase has seen motor manufacturers naming teams after themselves – Toyota, BMW, Honda. This is complete ownership.

All the way through this evolutionary process, team bosses have come and gone, and many have had to change utterly the way they work. What has gone by the way is the buccaneering spirit of the early days when Ken Tyrrell, Frank Williams and Bernie Ecclestone made wheeling and dealing into an art form. As soon as marketing men, chief financial officers and executive boards got involved, everything became a lot more rigid, predictable and, quite frankly, less fun. One man, however, has managed to keep this side of things going, even though he is (and is still considered to be) an outsider: Flavio Briatore. He has always been a salaried employee, first at Benetton, then at Renault, but has nevertheless managed to carve out enough operating space for himself to act like a constructor of old.

A hard core of these constructors are still in the sport. Max Mosley, who co-owned March, and Bernie Ecclestone, boss of Brabham, are still in the paddock of course. Ron Dennis has sold much of his team to Mercedes, and there are constant rumours that he is ready, if not willing, to sell them the rest. Frank Williams resisted being strong-armed by BMW and they parted ways. Eddie Jordan, Peter Sauber and Giancarlo Minardi all sold out. Now there are new bosses, some employed by the motor manufacturer, like Mario Theissen at BMW and Nick Fry at Honda, and some by outside companies, like Christian Horner at Red Bull Racing. Former driver Gerhard Berger owns 50 per cent of Toro Rosso. All are on the lookout for drivers, but have different agendas: some want the drivers to pay for their drive, some want to hire them; others have drivers 'suggested' to them by the engine manufacturers, sponsors and/or owners. It is a wide and varied mosaic, but I think it can be narrowed down to five main types of team boss (and consequently five different types of relationship with a driver): the father figure (Ron Dennis); the stern teacher (Frank Williams); the money maker (Eddie Jordan); the innovator (Flavio Briatore); and the next generation (Christian Horner).

'The key thing with Ron is his mentoring, this father figure he aspires to be,' said Anthony Rowlinson, the award-winning British journalist, formerly editor at *Autosport*, now at the *Red Bulletin*. 'And there are a few key drivers you can look at where this applies. The classic case is Mika Hakkinen. Ron mentored him into a double world champion from being a young and naive driver who was very quick, but who maybe did not have the full package of skills. Ron took him into the McLaren fold, nurtured him and took away all the distractions of being in this sport, allowing him to focus simply on being a driver. It was very much done in a fatherly way: "Come on board, my son. I'll take you on this journey with me." Mika has always been quite deferential to Ron.

'Ron has tried to achieve this success again, several times, with other drivers, and has possibly failed. The great counterpoint to Mika is Kimi Raikkonen, who succeeded Mika at McLaren. Again, he came in at a young age, and was a fast Finn, but he went against Ron's mentoring and they had two or three big fall-outs. There was one particular time when Ron disciplined Kimi over getting drunk away from races. People close to Kimi will say that the time Ron wrote that letter to Kimi was the final nail in the coffin in his relationship with McLaren and sent him to Ferrari. So Ron has experienced his mentoring style both ways. Once it was very successful, as Mika was very receptive; another time he was unsuccessful, as Kimi bristled. It will be fascinating to see what happens now that Ron has hired Lewis Hamilton, another young guy, and one who has been through the McLaren school from the age of eleven, when he first met Ron. Who knows if he will try to do the same thing, or how Lewis will respond. That will be a fascinating play to watch over the next four or five seasons.'

Ron Dennis has had two South American and two Finnish drivers. They were all very different from one another, but you get the impression that Dennis somehow stereotyped them in some sort of way. I remember a comment he made when told that Juan Pablo Montoya could be a bit of handful. He said that he had experience of South American drivers – not realising, perhaps, that the differences between a

Brazilian and a Colombian are quite stark, in terms both of language and culture. The two Finns also turned out to be quite different, in terms of character. So it will be interesting to see not only how Lewis Hamilton responds but also how Dennis interacts with Fernando Alonso. Rowlinson spotted them hugging at the last race of 2006 in Brazil, which for Dennis is quite a statement as he is fastidious about handshakes, never mind man-hugs. 'After Alonso had won the title, he was walking round the paddock with an Oviedo flag round his shoulders about ten minutes after the end of the race. The McLaren offices were next door to Renault's. Ron stepped out of his area, and they sort of clocked each other. Alonso walked up to him, gave him a man-hug and said to Ron, "There will be more of this next year, you'll see." You could see there was a bond already.' But Rowlinson is not optimistic about Dennis carrying on the father-figure thing with the Spaniard. 'In my opinion Alonso, who is a self-contained guy, will find it hard to accept a father-figure type role from Ron. It will be interesting to see how that pans out as Ron will have to put his own ego to one side and accept that the guy is good enough to win two world champs on his own without the super father figure above him.'

The body language in the McLaren pits will also be very interesting. In the past, Dennis has often stood next to his favourite driver as he is getting ready to drive, or he just stands next to his car as the engineers and mechanics are finalising preparations. It's his way of showing support, but it is quite destabilising for the other man driving for the team. He did this when Michael Andretti was trying to find his feet in F1: Dennis stood by Senna's car. Hakkinen, too, benefited from this minor form of favouritism. So who will get the 'treatment' in 2007, Hamilton or Alonso? And how will they react to it?

Jo Ramirez spent many years at McLaren and has had a grandstand view of how Dennis operates in relation to his drivers. I put it to him that Dennis developed into this father figure because he really admires, likes, and, in some cases, loves his drivers. 'Yes he does,' Ramirez agreed, 'because basically he is very much a racing man. Of course he's a very good businessman too, and he also has tremendous vision for how things are going to pan out, but basically he admires them very much. McLaren has never had an official number one driver, as other teams have. But he stopped Coulthard twice that I know of. He does get very involved with his drivers, and Mika had been let down a few times by the car, so in Jerez in 1997 he asked David to let Mika pass him. The Finn had nearly stopped and David had passed, though he should have been behind him, and that is when Ron got involved, telling him to drop back. Ron felt that Mika was overdue a win and, though he was not the number one driver, he had nevertheless been there before David, so Ron felt that he should be allowed his first win. It was a bit of psychology, so that he would have two race winners for the next season. The other time was in Australia in 1998. Mika misheard something on his radio and thought the team had told him to come into the pits when we hadn't. They both slowed down, David right on the pit straight, and it looked very bad.'

I have categorised Frank Williams as the 'stern teacher' mainly because his team seems to have a 'my way or the highway' approach to drivers. Wonderfully successful, Williams is an engaging, polite, smiling man, and it is hard to see him as one who fires world champions willy-nilly, has he has done over the years. Maybe the clue is in the full name of the team: Williams Grand Prix Engineering. Perhaps the focus is on the technical side rather than the human.

'For so long the team was so good he could afford to lose world champions,' Rowlinson pointed out. 'When Damon [Hill] won the title in 1996, with all due respect, he was not the greatest F1 driver ever, yet he was able to win a title in the Williams because the car was so far ahead of the competition. Damon was the classic example of a driver being dumped when Frank decided he was not good enough. Then he won the title, but Frank had taken his decision about a year before and he was not going to backtrack. Damon was out, and that was it. In terms of lacking sentiment about drivers Frank must be the ultimate example of a guy who sees a driver as just a bloke who is part of the car. It was great to have that attitude when they were so successful, but he can't really afford to do that any more. Now he has Nico Rosberg, who is effectively still a rookie, and Alex Wurz, who is probably at best second- or third-choice driver for many people. These are not the great days of the Williams driver line-ups, with Alain Prost, then Ayrton Senna, and all the other great champions they have had. If I were Frank I would be thinking about treating the drivers much better and giving them the best possible environment in which to flourish, not just come down on them as hard as he can and force them to survive, which seems to be his rationale.' Still, Rowlinson and a great many other people have much sympathy for Williams because he came through the ranks the hard way. 'We all know the story about collecting the twopence pieces so he could make calls from the phone box outside his office, as he could not pay the phone bills. His was a hard way into motor racing, so he probably feels that he does not owe anyone anything, least of all namby-pamby racing drivers who are bloody lucky to drive his car. That is where he starts and finishes. That is his mindset, and probably always will be.'

Nico Rosberg, who started the 2006 season really well, faded over the distance, and it could be that once again Williams might not be the right kind of environment for this kind of young driver. 'I spoke to Keke [Rosberg] at the first race of the year,' Ian Phillips told me, 'and I said, "You don't know how lucky you were getting your boy into Williams rather than having to put him with us [Midland]." And he said, "I sat there yesterday in Malaysia. The kid's never been to the circuit before, and he said Williams are so inflexible, they wouldn't let him out just for one lap. I think that's wrong. I had to bite my tongue. My wife copped it from me on the phone that night. The team won't let the boy out." If you're taking a new boy, you can't say "We're Williams, we're the best." The guy has to have a feel of the place; you can't get it off a few games on PlayStation. You've got to give him a three-lap run, a five-lap run, just so he really knows where the contours of the place are.'

Ramirez agrees that at Williams drivers are just 'another company employee. Which is surprising. Why the hell do they pay them so much money then? At McLaren the drivers are always treated as special people. If you are treated like that, when you get into the car you are more relaxed and you perform better. You don't have to worry about anything else because it has all been taken care of. To me that's very important. At Williams they didn't do things like that, though things might have changed now. Friendships are important, and even though he was at Williams and I was at McLaren, Ayrton always asked me to fly in his helicopter after races. It was a nice gesture which came out of the friendship we developed at McLaren, where he was treated very well.'

Ramirez recalled the time when Williams let Damon Hill go after he won the world title. 'He asked for too much money,' he said. 'I can't remember how the conversation went, but Frank said to Damon that he twice lost him the world championship, or something like that. He's just very tough. On the other hand Damon maybe got a little bit too self-important when he won the championship, because he wanted far too much money. We offered him a contract too, so he could come to McLaren, which I thought was fantastic, but he didn't think it was good enough, that it did not reflect his position as a world champion. It was very good money, but it was performance-related, which Ron always liked to do. Damon knew that Adrian Newey was coming to McLaren, knew how good Newey was at making a winning car, so I'm sure he regretted it bitterly afterwards. He went to Arrows for £4 million. He would have got a lot more money at Williams or at McLaren, but he refused them both and had to take what was left.

'So many drivers have made wrong choices. But he still had some good driving in him. In Hungary he was leading the race at one point. He had passed Schumacher, and then finished second, which in that car was quite brilliant. I was happy for him because he was a nice man, very generous. After the Hungary GP I always used to go to my place in southern France. I usually used to get a lift with Senna back to England Sunday night and then take a plane on Monday morning to France. But I found out that Damon had hired a summerhouse for his family near Nice. So I asked Damon, "Are you going to Nice after the race?" He said, "Yes." I said, "Have you got a place for me?" He said, "Yes, I'll give you a lift." It was a small plane and they didn't really have the space. There were already quite a few of them: Damon, his manager, Pedro Diniz, and somebody else. But it was fantastic, and Damon was so hospitable. We drank a lot of champagne. Yes, he was all right as a person, but he made the wrong decision.'

Eddie Jordan was the consummate wheeler-dealer. He had already made quite a bit of money out of the sport even before he came into F1 through his driver management company. I remember getting a call out of the blue from him when I was with the *Sunday Times*. He introduced himself, mentioned Bernie Ecclestone a few times, then offered me the opportunity to interview this hot new driver of his called Jean Alesi, who was going to be a world champion. So a few days later I was sitting cross-legged in Jordan's back garden in

Oxford's elegant Summertown talking to a shy and smiling Alesi while all around us Jordan offspring were engaged in a chaotic picnic party. Later, when Jordan himself entered F1, he made sure I always remembered that he had given me the first exclusive Alesi interview. 'I own you' became a catchphrase of his. And it was uttered only half in jest.

'Eddie had a good eye for talent,' Ramirez continued. 'Look at some of the quick guys who have passed through his team, like Giancarlo Fisichella, Jarno Trulli, Michael Schumacher, Jean Alesi, and many more. Because he was a racer himself, and did pretty well in F3 – he could have gone further with a bit of extra funding and different breaks – he wasn't a team owner like some of the others who just took the cash. Look at Minardi when they took that Israeli guy [Chanoch Nissany, in 2005]; one practice session and it was clear he was not remotely capable of driving an F1 car. Or take Alex Yoong. People like that – total pay drivers. He tried never to descend to that level. Maybe it was the racer in him, but he was always on the lookout for talent. Even in 2003 when he had Ralph Firman in one car, a pay driver who was not quite good enough, it helped pay the way for Giancarlo Fisichella in the other car. So Eddie liked the money, but he also wanted the glamorous quick guy in the car as well.'

Flavio Briatore is the innovator. He arrived on the F1 scene in the mid-1980s, parachuted in by the Benetton family who wanted a trusted hand at the helm of the newly acquired F1 team. The Benetton brothers had initially asked him to head the launch of the Italian clothes shops in North America. He opened 800 shops, a feat that has led him repeatedly to comment that F1 is not as complicated as people make it out to be. He soon befriended Bernie Ecclestone and the two became inseparable business partners in F1 for many years. Still close now, they are always ready to shake up the more conservative elements of the sport. He is generally quite disparaging of the other team bosses and has shown with facts that not only is he the best there is in the paddock, on a relatively small budget compared to some of the other teams, he also set new standards for the training and recruitment of drivers.

'He has re-set the mould,' Rowlinson concurred. 'He seems to groom drivers so perfectly, whether it's his hands-off approach or his ability to spot talent and then nurture it. Fernando Alonso is the recent example, and Michael Schumacher before that. He is able to understand what a racing driver is and seems to recognise the mental side as well. In 2002, when he had Trulli and Button in the team, he let Button go, even though the Englishman was clearly a talented young prospect. At the time he said, "That boy will never be a world champion." He replaced him with Fernando Alonso. It was ruthless and brutal, but absolutely right in the way he identified the right thing to do. He seems to have an instinctive understanding of what it takes to have the total package as a driver. He has recognised it in a number of guys.'

Briatore himself is very clear about his management style as it is applied to drivers. 'Take the right decisions, and stick with them,' he stated, even though it might land you in hot water, as he described in chapter 5. As well as for letting

Button go, he was also criticised in 2006 for allowing Alonso to go to McLaren. Again he is very clear. 'I'm not here to block people's careers,' he said. 'Alonso has chosen his new path for sporting reasons. Renault could not give a guarantee that it would be racing in 2008. McLaren offered him a three-year deal.' Like Ecclestone, Briatore is very pragmatic and will not fight wars he cannot win, and he believes in letting his drivers get on with it. He told me he never reads their interviews and says that he gives them as much decision space as they need. He cites Mark Webber as an example: 'I offered him a drive at Renault, but he preferred to stay at Williams. He could have been Fisi's team-mate, but he stuck to Williams. This is to show I don't interfere with my drivers. Both are signed to my management company, Alonso up to 2010 or 2011.' Webber's move to Red Bull Racing for 2007 was also orchestrated by Briatore, which the Australian acknowledges with gratitude.

Rowlinson sees the Italian's success as coming from the consistency of management he brings to his teams, where the key people have been the same for many years. 'If you look at the success of Benetton in the mid-1990s, and more recently at Renault, he seems to apply the same principles all the way through. Guys like [director of engineering] Pat Symonds have stuck with the team for a long time. They always say what a great manager Flav is. Pat has been there since the Toleman days. It seems Flav allows people to do their jobs well, having identified the right people for the job in the first place. Maybe it's because he's not a petrol-head that he can see what it takes to be a good driver, a successful one, and is able to pick the right guys. It is a successful team, and people stay there. It has happened twice now [with Schumacher and Alonso], so it can't be a fluke.' And there is a third talent perhaps on the way to greatness. Heikki Kovalainen, another young Finnish prodigy, has been brought straight into the world championship-winning team for 2007 by Briatore. That is a big statement, but then again, as he says himself, Briatore's strike rate is pretty high. A betting man would put money on that combination to win in the near future.

'I like Flavio as a person,' Jo Ramirez commented, 'and, from the very start, from when he first came into F1, he was a businessman. He said, "If I make a pound at the end of the year, then that's good, and if I've enjoyed myself and if I haven't lost, that's fine, I'll do it again next year. The first time I lose a pound, then it's no good." It's such a totally different approach from the other managers, and it's been good. He's brought some flamboyant spirit to the paddock. Life is too short. You've got to enjoy it.'

Christian Horner is the impossibly fresh-faced young man in charge of Red Bull Racing. Indeed, he is positively childlike if we take into consideration the fact that he also runs a GP2 team as well as an A1 outfit. He himself raced to a good standard, reaching F3000, though that was his limit, as he readily admits. He always looks relaxed, has a kind word to say to everyone he meets, and generally exudes an air of total confidence. But he has a tough job, as Red Bull has invested lots of money into the team, including buying the very expensive services of Adrian Newey, who has taken over from John Barnard as the must-have accessory for any ambitious team in the paddock.

'He has a very good ability to judge what makes a driver good,' Anthony Rowlinson said. 'He can talk very intelligently about drivers. Many team bosses might ask, "Is that driver quick? Is he good?" And in most cases they can't judge the mechanics and the technique themselves. But some team principals can. Eddie Jordan probably could, while Frank Williams probably couldn't. Christian definitely can. If you talk to him about what makes a driver quick, about corner entering and all that, he can talk at length about it. He goes and watches drivers on track and assesses their abilities.'

I have never seen him on track in that context, but I have overheard Horner talking about drivers to McLaren's Martin Whitmarsh, the CEO of the F1 team. Just a casual chat in the paddock, both men angling to see what the other knew of certain young drivers, with Whitmarsh wondering if Horner might be doing any tests in the near future, and Horner inviting the McLaren man to send one of his protégés to test with him. All very cool, but all very meaningful. Information is vital in the fast-moving business of F1 and any interesting young prospect is rapidly evaluated by those in the know. And clearly Horner is one whose judgement is highly valued.

Another time I eavesdropped on a conversation between Horner and a young driver at a function. It sounds intrusive, but that was not the point of my listening. It was the subject matter that interested me, for the young driver was asking the team boss about his driving, how he could improve, where he could find more consistency, and how he could manage the car better. Horner was encyclopaedic, clear and helpful. And very impressive. The next generation.

And finally, a man whose attitude, Rowlinson feels, is different from that of all the other team principals. He's not a team boss, but he was one once. He was also a driver manager, so he knows and understands the spectrum of driver requirements. 'Bernie Ecclestone's take on drivers is based on how good they are going to be for the show,' Rowlinson said. 'He does not worry too much about how good they are, as long as there are enough top guys at the front of the grid. Bringing back Villeneuve in 2004 is an example of this. Jacques was largely past his best, but the move generated lots of headlines about F1, as did bringing Montoya over from the US. I'm sure he said to Frank Williams, "We have to have this guy, he's making all the headlines in the US." So Montoya comes over and is an instant success. We all remember his overtaking of Schumacher at Interlagos that year. In the end he wasn't quite as successful as his talent merited, but there is no doubt Bernie has an understanding of what a headline-grabbing driver is. He moaned about Alonso's attitude after he won his first title, saying he wasn't doing enough to big up the fact he was world champion. Bernie doesn't just respect Alonso for being a good driver, he wants him to be the superstar as well, something Alonso has always resisted.'

Thus the views of the Padre Padrone, the Boss of Bosses, for the whole of the sport.

CHAPTER TEN

THE PRESIDENT ON DRIVERS

Max Mosley has been involved in motor racing since the early 1960s when, after graduating in physics from Christ Church, Oxford, and then qualifying as a solicitor from Gray's Inn, he started to take part in club events. In 1968 he began racing in F2, eventually pairing up with Piers Courage in the Williams team. But, like so many of the top people in motor racing, and F1 in particular, he soon swapped his race overalls for a shirt and tie, and in 1969 he started March Engineering with Robin Herd, Alan Rees and Graham Coaker. Mosley's time as a constructor was fruitful: he won a number of races in F2 and F1, and in Indy Cars; Jackie Stewart, Ronnie Petersen and Vittorio Brambilla were all winners in the 1970s. But as the political and legal battles flared for control of F1 in the latter years of the 1970s and the early part of the following decade, Mosley increasingly found himself alongside Bernie Ecclestone and the other constructors in a legal advisory capacity. He quit March and in 1991 was elected president of the FIA, the sport's governing body. Since then he has been elected three more times.

Mosley knows motor racing from every conceivable angle: as a driver, a constructor, a legislator, and even from the high-tech end through founding the consultancy Simtek Research. He was key to the drafting of the Concorde Agreement, which still holds together the squabbling tribes of the paddock, and also to the introduction of a raft of safety measures. Here are the president's thoughts. For one with a such a strong and ongoing legal background, he can be quite indiscreet and will often say something very juicy, only to gently remind the interviewer that 'of course I would not like this to be quoted'. Frustrating for the writer, but fun to listen to.

Firstly, I asked him what he thought were the essentials that must come together to make a top racing driver, no matter in what formula or decade. Like so many other F1 people (see chapter 2) he cited speed, but, as with so many things he says, he managed to find a twist which then questioned many widely held assumptions. 'All drivers in F1 are very, very fast,' he began. 'Indeed, many outside F1 are also very fast, but that of course is not enough to make them into a success. It is only when they combine several aspects of character in one person that they start to become a winner. Speed is very important, but possibly not the most important factor, because no one would say that Alain Prost or Niki Lauda were really, really quick drivers. The British magazine *F1 Racing* sent out a questionnaire asking who was the quickest driver in F1 over the past 50 years, and I would be surprised if Prost or Lauda featured on those lists, yet between them they won seven world championships.

'The other thing to look for is intelligence, and character, in the sense of not being downcast by little failures, and not being stopped by setbacks. The best example of this was Michael Schumacher in 2006. It did not matter what was thrown at him or how upset he was privately – and I believe he was very fragile privately – he was absolutely resolute in the face of great adversity. For example, when they put him at the back of the grid in Monaco he did the impossible and came through to finish in fifth place. And consider when he had those reverses in Brazil, in the last race of the season … after the second one almost any other driver would have given up and cruised round to happy retirement. But it simply was not what he was going to do. He fought back.

'So many of the drivers I've had dealings with were fragile psychologically. We had one driver who was very good in F1, but truly outstanding in F2. What you had to do with him, when he went out for the first practice, you had to tell him he was quickest when he wasn't. He might have been about twelfth. But next time he went out he would be quickest. We just needed to psych him up. Then you had someone like Chris Amon who never won a race but who was a very quick driver but maybe lacked some of the other components. So, drivers need intelligence, they need speed, and they need determination and a willingness not to be downcast by difficulty. And all these things need to be combined. And I think in many ways that this is probably true of most top sportsmen. When I watch a tennis match, though I'm not much of a tennis fan, if something is manifestly wrong, if I were a tennis player I would just walk off. But of course they don't; they just pull themselves together and get on with it. It really takes a special kind of person to persevere in adversity.'

Mosley then explored a difficult area which Jackie Stewart also tried to define – the seeming ability of top drivers to master time. 'For anyone who races at all successfully, everything slows down, and you see things that you should not see. You notice individual people in the crowd – all drivers will say that – and it just doesn't feel that fast. When you first get into a racing car, you find that the first couple of laps, if you have not driven for a week, feel amazingly fast. It all seems amazingly fast. Then you push through the feeling that this is completely stupid compared to the road, it settles down, and it becomes completely natural. You suddenly have plenty of time. Time slows down. And I think this is more or less true of all drivers above good club level. If you get in your road car after that it all feels so soft, gentle and slow, even if it's a high-performance car. The racing car is just another world.'

I wondered if Mosley thought that driving at the top level was a skill that could be taught. Mosley said yes, but only up to a point. 'You can probably teach most fit young men, or women, especially if you had simulators and such things. You can teach them to get very, very close to the lap times of the top drivers, but it's the last bit that is very difficult. What is the last bit? I would say a second a lap, but it depends on the car. If the car is easy to drive then the gaps between the drivers come down, especially if you remove the tasks they have to do – and in a modern F1 car you have removed lots of tasks, despite my best endeavours, certainly compared to GP2. Nowadays you don't have to worry about the clutch, or missing a gear. All you have to do is flick the paddle on the steering wheel at the right moment and it will change gear. But all of those things enable the lesser driver to get close to the quicker one. The top drivers are always going to be quickest – at least that is their view. I remember once having a long discussion with Michael Schumacher about electronic aids, as it has always been a debating point, at least in my mind. Conventional thinking is that we should do away with them as this is a human sport and we should not be driven by computers. But privately I have often wondered if this is actually right, and Schumacher's view – though he didn't quite put it like this – was that no matter how many electronic aids there were he reckoned the fastest driver would still be the fastest. All the technology does is narrow down the gap. So I do think you can teach them. Just as you can teach a significant number of young men to be modern fighter pilots. Not everybody can do it, but a significant number can. But there will still be a few people who do that bit better.'

So, if teaching is an option, it is an unrealistic one. Besides, this is such an expensive sport to get into that there isn't a proper selection process, at least not an equitable one. The drivers who make it to the top are mostly from moneyed backgrounds. 'It's true that one of the biggest problems in motor sport is that you need so much money to start,' Mosley concurred. 'But it's interesting that there is a significant number of what you might call working-class, or certainly not wealthy, drivers: Mika Hakkinen, Kimi Raikkonen, Fernando Alonso and, of course, Michael Schumacher spring immediately to mind. All people with no money [when they started] but gifted with supreme talent. Someone will notice them and back them. They'll be doing their bit in karting, and they'll just stand out. These are just four off the top of my head.' With the mention of those three multiple world champions, and one who might still do it, the rich-boy argument went up in flames. Cream rises to the top, was what Mosley was saying.

Still, the point that it is a rich man's sport is still a valid one, and one, in the wider context, with which Mosley agrees. 'I keep telling all the clubs around the world, they must encourage karting and they must do so with a single-engine and single-make series – single everything. It has to become as cheap as possible. You have to spread the net as wide as possible and then the talent will come in. You have only to look at skiing. Look at Austria, with eight million people the top skiing nation, and compare poor old UK with 60 million people. There is nothing inherently different; there are no mental or physical differences in the human talent. You would find a large number of brilliant skiers in the UK if they all started at the age of two, as the Austrians do. It's simply a question of opportunity, and this is a big problem in motor sport. Think how many Michael Schumachers there are walking around China, some who have not even driven a car yet. It's a problem we have and one we talk a lot about, and we have not solved it yet.'

Another area that has exercised Mosley's mind over the years is safety. He has done an awful lot to minimise the risk of accidents in motor racing and has taken this stance with road cars too. The FIA is very active in this area, and I put it to him that there is a strange schizophrenia in motor sport, and

F1 in particular, as a lot of people are attracted to the sport because it is dangerous and a big shunt could happen. The fans, at least a great many of them, are there to experience the frisson when things start to unravel on the track. 'There is an element of that,' Mosley conceded, 'because even if it isn't as dangerous as it was, it still feels dangerous. And it does not feel any different to drive an older car than it does a modern one. The only difference would be when you went off. When I raced, the cars were made from space frame, like bicycle tubing, and the petrol tanks, which were made of thin aluminium, were kept in place with tie-wraps – no rubber or anything like that. And these cars would go at 160mph or 170mph, and you would race somewhere where there was the road, a bit of grass and the trees. It was completely, utterly mad by modern standards, but if you said to any of the current F1 drivers "You can race like that or not race at all", I'm not sure that one of them would say no. Maybe some of the older ones might, but not when they were young. Take David Coulthard – I think he would say no. But when he was starting out he raced like we all raced, and that's that. Drivers have that mentality, and I think people realise that.

'We will never stop the shunts in F1, because if you are going to do any sport at the limit of your ability you will make mistakes yourself. And then, as it's motor racing, you have mechanical failure to contend with, other people's mistakes, and so on. So there will always be the shunts. For me, it is important that the drivers walk away and, funnily enough, I'm sure it's the same for the spectators. So they take the risk, they walk on the high wire, but, in the end, however flimsy it is, there's a safety net that just stops them from getting hurt. I think the public appreciates this.'

Danger and fear are words (and feelings) that go together. For this book, and over the years, I have spoken to many people on this subject. As I've said, it is the one area in motor sport where people are mostly coy and reluctant to come clean. It is easier to talk about, and get answers on, the most secretive of contracts than it is to get F1 people to open up about their fears when in or around an F1 car. Mosley, however, is more candid than most. He turned his thoughts to one of the drivers who, especially for the 1960s generation, was one of the beacons for all that was daring and over the top in motor racing.

'One of the quickest drivers of all time was Jochen Rindt,' Mosley said. 'He was the king of F2. He was also brilliant in F1 – he won the world championship in his last year [1970] – but he really was the king of F2. That is the formula I was also racing in. I remember talking to him about Monza, which in those days had no chicanes, so you would come to the Parabolica and go past that straight by the pits, and where there is now the chicane there was the Curva Grande, a long, long, long right-hander. In an F2 car in those days it was allegedly flat. I don't believe it was, because you'd follow someone who was a fast driver and you would have to lift, though I take into consideration you'd be in the tow. So I was saying to Rindt, "I find it really, really difficult to take the Curva Grande flat. At the last minute, I just have a little breather, then in." So he asked, "Why is that?" I said, "Well, I think to myself, what if someone has blown their engine just in front of me? Or what if something has gone wrong and I hit a patch of oil? I'm going to be in the trees." And he looked at me and said, "If you think like that you shouldn't be racing." I always thought like that, but to him it was different. When you got to the grid at the end of the old-style qualifying laps, and there were 40 cars and only 22 places, you just bloody well took it flat. Mike Hawthorn used to say about one of those corners – not that one, just one of those really tough corners – "Every time I was going into it, someone bigger than me lifted my foot." Self-preservation, you see. If you talked to Brabham, he would say you could not afford to have accidents in his day as the chances of getting killed were very high. One in every eight accidents in the 1960s resulted in death or serious injury. Now it's something like one in every 500. So you tried not to have an accident.'

I pressed him to define the fear a driver feels. 'Fear is very hard to describe,' he said. 'It's not fear like you grit your teeth and do it. Fear is the wrong word. I'd rather call it "an appreciation of risk". It is a form of fear. Like a soldier who is going into battle. We all have that; it's part of the human make-up when you are putting yourself in a dangerous situation. It's a little bit different from fear as in the anxiety sense. It's not fear of the unknown. If you put me in a submarine 500 feet underwater and started dropping depth charges, well, I would still do my job but, Christ, I wouldn't like it; I would find that frightening. If the water is going to come rushing in, you have no control, you know? Whereas in a racing car, until whatever is going to happen has happened you have a degree of control, you are doing something. Suddenly something goes wrong – you have a mechanical failure or something. Then it all seems to happen in slow-motion, but there is no time to be frightened because you have to do whatever you have to do and be ready to take whatever action you can. In the old days that meant letting off the fire extinguisher at the right moment, that sort of thing.'

Racing fans always marvel at racing drivers who have had an accident – say at the start, usually quite spectacular and very frightening to witness – but who just get out of their cars and rush back to the pits for the spare car, running with that ungainly gait caused by helmets, HANS devices and uncomfortable flame-retardant suits. If they can, if they are allowed, they will be back in that cockpit come what may. Are they crazy? Do they have no feelings? 'If you have an incident on the road,' Mosley explained, 'if you're just driving along and something unexpected happens, most people will be shaken. It's a form of shock. And they might be shaken up for some considerable time afterwards. That would happen to me if I were involved in an accident, even if I wasn't hurt. But in a race car it has absolutely no effect whatsoever. You spin, you go off, whatever. As long as you don't hurt yourself, you want to go again. It's because you are so pumped with adrenalin before you even start that you don't get a sudden release of it. In a road car you are calm, then suddenly there is a massive release of adrenalin and it shakes you up. In the race car, pumped up beforehand, you can spin at 150mph, come to rest, fire up the car and go. You just don't think about it. But all this is easy to say. I never really hurt myself in a race car. If you hurt yourself, it might be different. But again, it requires no imagination at all. You can absolutely picture the scene. The bright lights, the smell of disinfectant – you can see it all without it ever having happened.'

I've always thought of drivers as quite lonely figures. Out there they're on their own, insulated from the world around them by the noise of the car, the visual impediment of the helmet. Just them and a brutal machine that has been put together by others on which they have to rely utterly. There can never be room for any doubt that the car will always do absolutely what it is meant to do, under very heavy stresses and loads. Some of the people who assemble and work on the car the drivers see every race in the pits; others he may never see. So, do drivers ever worry about how good their team is, in this sense? 'You never start thinking that the garage employees are second-rate mechanics and they are going to leave something undone,' Mosley said, 'although it can happen. But anyone who has done much racing will have experienced failure from mechanical error. It's one of those things – something breaks and you're in trouble. How bad depends on where it happens on the circuit. The other side of all this is that the right driver will motivate the team, and of course the primary example of that is Michael Schumacher. He did that to an extraordinary degree.

'And another thing: all the top drivers, without exception, are really good complainers. Jackie Stewart was famous for this. When he won the championship, the tyre company would ring up to say well done and he would start complaining about the tyres. It's constant pressure to improve, on every single person connected to your car. That is the characteristic of all top drivers.'

This, Mosley added, is a form of cleverness. There are drivers who are more clever than others. He mentioned a couple, both fast, charming, 'really nice people, ones you were always pleased to bump into in the street. But both were blindingly thick. They had extraordinary talent – you could see it every time it rained – but speed was all they had. They just were not clever. They won very few races and didn't really leave the kind of mark on the sport they should have. Then again, there is a difference between intelligence and sensitivity. Some drivers are very good at picking up what the car is doing. I believe Riccardo Patrese was very good at this. Other drivers simply drive round the problem. In the old days you were reliant on the driver to analyse what was wrong with the car, because until someone told you what was wrong with it you couldn't put it right. So the engineers would go corner by corner, asking the driver what the car was doing, but some drivers could recite it, some could not. And some of the very best drivers, when they had a problem with the car they would simply drive round it and nearly not know they'd had it. That was a big issue in the 1970s. Today they have 300 or 400 channels of info. They know practically everything the car is doing at all times. The only thing they need from the driver is how he feels, if he feels more comfortable with solution A or B. Because if he feels more comfortable, he will go quicker.'

The president of the FIA has known many drivers and has had unrivalled access to them, often in social situations where they are naturally less guarded than in the midst of a media scrum after qualifying. I wondered which were his stand-out drivers of all time. 'Well, before my time I'd say Stirling Moss and Juan Manuel Fangio, possibly Alberto Ascari. Since I've been involved, Jochen Rindt, Ronnie Peterson, Ayrton Senna and Michael Schumacher – they would probably be the ones.' Was there a common trait in all these drivers? 'They are all racer's racers, in the sense that they were all blindingly quick. Then they have other characteristics as well, hence the success. I admire them because they do the bit that counts really well. When I say "counts", I don't mean in the sense of success, but what really counts if you're assessing a racing driver as a pure driver. Senna was amazing when he did a qualifying lap. Schumacher was extraordinary when the pressure was on. Peterson was just an amazing talent. And Rindt was unbelievably quick when he felt like it, which was not all that often. But when he did, my goodness.

'Take two little things about Rindt, for example. At Monaco in 1970 he realised he was catching Brabham and just went God knows how much faster in the last three laps of the race having been on the same tyres all the way through the race. I talked to him after the race and said to him, "That was just amazing." He said, "There's only been two times in my life when I've gone absolutely flat out, and that was one of them, and I don't like doing it." I wanted to know when the other one was. "Zolder, in 1968," said Rindt. Well, that for me was a big thing as I was in that race in 1968 and there was an incident at the start, one of those things when there is bodywork, dust and confusion everywhere. Somehow I avoided all of that, and then we were off racing. And after seven or eight laps I saw a blue flag. "That's not possible," I thought. It meant one of the leaders was catching me up. But there was no way in the world someone could have caught me after eight laps, however quick they were going at the front. I looked in the mirrors and saw it was Rindt, and I thought, "What the fuck is he doing there?" What had happened was that someone had hit him up the back at the start. He had been in pole position, so he had spun and had to start behind everybody else, and now he was coming though the field. There were two very fast right-handers out the back in Zolder. On one of them he went round the outside of me. I thought I was on the limit, and I could see his hand working away as he went past me. It was just unbelievable. I thought that I would never be able to do that. It was just like watching someone on another planet. So I was fascinated to hear him say that after the Monaco race. He was just extraordinary like that.

'Peterson was also exceptional in that sense. He could, if he felt like it, drive beautifully, and in a bad car, like the March 701, the car we had in our first year. He would come round the old Woodcote, under the Daily Express Bridge, and then all the way round. He would keep it flat, and then, because the car would start to go, put it on to opposite lock, his arms crossed of course, then take away the outside arm, and with the thumb take the steering wheel to the stops. He would hold it like that, still flat and still with one wheel more or less on the grass. It was awesome to watch and there was no one else who could do that. He was in a shit car in our team and there was Lauda, admittedly early in his career, in the same car. Ronnie would not complain, but Lauda would complain, quite rightly, about the car. Petersen would be one and a half seconds quicker, just from sheer amazing driving talent. Senna and Schumacher later on, they could have done the same.'

CHAPTER ELEVEN

SNAPSHOTS

I would like to end this short look at what makes racing drivers so special by sharing some moments I and other F1 people spent with them, and some of the things they said in more informal situations. These are just snapshots, in no particular order. Many involve Ayrton Senna, partly because I was both a journalist and then a McLaren team employee when he was driving, and also because he was often surprising in his actions and words, and indeed controversial too. He could be ruthless, a fact to which a number of incidents involving team-mates testify, but of course he was also a devout Christian. Some people found this hard to take, and he was teased behind his back. He was different, for sure, and, from a journalist's viewpoint, quite a hard man to interview as you never knew which Senna would turn up.

I know for a fact that he disliked the media intensely. He was once having an argument with Ron Dennis, his team boss at McLaren, during his last stint there before going to Williams. Their relationship was quite fraught by then, certainly up and down. I was working at McLaren at the time and was standing with them as the spat developed. At one stage Dennis mentioned that one of their points of contention had been written about, as if to confirm it was true. 'How can you say that?' interrupted Senna. 'You hate the journalists as much as I do. You have no respect for them.' There were other instances like that, yet he would often sit and take time to explain things. For him it was a matter of respect.

This became very clear to me one day in his Honda motor home. Senna had been gruff all day with the press, and he was 'hiding' as his more usual berth would have been McLaren. Three of us, all journalists, were there too, writing and translating the engine manufacturer's press release. Because we were 'working' for Honda at the time, or at least for the few minutes it took us to do the job, we wouldn't have dreamt of doing any of those beastly journalistic things, like interview him. If we did speak to him it was about the weather or the food. Mostly, he kept his counsel. But on this day the veteran English journalist Denis Jenkinson came to sit with him. A Mille Miglia winner with Stirling Moss, 'Jenks' had written a great book called *Racing Driver*, published in 1959, which Senna had read. Now he was talking to the Brazilian about his own driving techniques for an update on the book. Senna's body language and tone of voice were so different from the ones we normally saw. Relaxed, friendly, courteous, even a little deferential, he clearly loved talking to the impish, bearded Jenks. This was not a 'journalist' as classified by him in his usual dealings with the press. This was someone he admired and respected, and he was happy to give as much of his time as was needed.

Respect is usually earned the hard way with racing drivers. They are doing something so different from everyone else that they do find it hard to empathise with mere scribblers and sponsor's agents, for example. Wearing the team uniform did put me in a different place as far as the drivers were concerned, however, and I managed to speak, or listen, in a different way to them. For example, I once came across Senna sitting outside the motor home after a test session. He looked tired, which was unusual for him, and I remarked on this. It was hard to drive the car, he said. This was the period when McLaren ran a Ford engine, and the whole team, not just Senna, was finding it hard to come to grips with the new power unit after the halcyon days with Honda. But I sensed this was more than just adapting to a new engine. I pressed him further. He gave me a long look, as if to decide whether he could speak to me, whether indeed I would understand what he had to say. Then he started one of his long monologues, delivered in that quiet voice of his, with the Brazilian lilt still affecting his vowels.

He told me he hated driving the car. That the car was shit – the only swear word he'd ever use, though he did use it a lot. It was shit to drive – I think he even said dangerous – and the engine was not fast or powerful enough. The result, he said, was that he had to drive at his maximum every time he got into the car, and that's how accidents happen. He told me he was on his limit, sometimes beyond, and he had to take the car way past its limits. And this was just to get a decent time, not a great one. That's when he told me a driver should always drive within himself, say at 80 per cent, so he always had something in reserve, mentally and physically, when it was needed. It was not possible to drive as if it was a qualifying lap, which he was a master of, in a race situation, lap after lap, for the whole race. And race after race. It was exhausting, he said.

Later that year McLaren struck a deal with Peugeot for a works engine. I was in the people carrier in Paris when Ron Dennis called Senna to tell him about the deal. That day the Brazilian had tested a McLaren which had been fitted with a Lamborghini V12. Chrysler, owners of the Italian engine makers, had asked for an independent evaluation of the engine's capability and potential. Senna loved the engine and told Dennis. This was a bit awkward, as the Peugeot deal had been struck. The embarrassed silence in the car was pretty loud, as these things can be. The fallout with Chrysler-Lamborghini has been well documented, and Lamborghini had to close down its engine-making factory. The Peugeot relationship turned out to be a disaster. Who knows what would have happened had Senna stayed to drive the Lamborghini engine, which he really liked.

That was also the period when Senna was a race-by-race paid driver. He and Dennis could not agree a contract, and Senna's problem at the time, which he told a number of people, was that he felt the McLaren 'package' was not good enough for him to commit wholeheartedly. The 'package' referred to by drivers is the relationship between chassis, engine and tyres, as well as the way the team interacts and the degree of sponsor involvement. Senna had been with McLaren all through his world titles, when he had pretty much the perfect package, including a team-mate in Alain Prost who pushed him all the way. Now things were very different, and he and Dennis were locked in prolonged discussions.

One time, on my way to my office at McLaren, I saw Senna sitting on a hard-backed chair in the corridor-cum-walkway outside Dennis's office at the old HQ in Woking. He looked like a naughty schoolboy who had been banished by the teacher. I suppose it was the hard-backed chair that did it; there was an area two steps further on with some easy chairs, where people normally waited to see the McLaren boss. The oddness of the sight – this was, after all, a three-time world champion, at the time the best of the best – was compounded by the fact that he was sitting upright, very stiffly, with his hands in front of him, cradling a large bound book. Instinctively, I knew it was a bible. He was totally absorbed in it, head down. I and many other people walked past, many times. Sometimes he would raise his head and smile, other times he did not. I can't remember how many hours he sat there, and I presume he went in to see Dennis a few times, but the sight of him sitting there has stayed with me all these years. It was a statement by him, I suppose. That he had patience, that he had value, that he could be humble, that he felt the time was worth investing. I also wondered if just through his sheer presence he was putting Dennis under pressure, as everyone in the factory would have known he was there and might have interpreted Senna's vigil in the corridor as a commitment to deliver for the team; the only question was, did the team want him? Of course, the workforce loved Senna, even though they often saw the haughty side of him. Wins meant bonuses for many, a good feeling for all, and job security. They would not have swapped him for anyone else.

At the Hockenheimring Senna once asked me if I wanted a ride back to the hotel in Heidelberg. I said yes, and we got into a Mercedes he had for the weekend. He then started to drive towards the exit of the circuit. The main road is shared by cars and spectators, except at peak times. The Germans love motor racing, and the circuit and access roads at and around Hockenheim are always crowded with people. Senna drove swiftly out of the car park, then faster and faster, sliding past pedestrians and other cars very smoothly. Being driven by racing drivers is always a little nerve-racking as their timing and sense of space really is different from lesser mortals. So I was feeling a little tense, but, hey, this is Ayrton Senna! Who was I to worry or even dare say something?

Suddenly a policeman jumped into the middle of the road, waving his hands in the air and looking very angry. Then, sort of at the same time, another approached the passenger window and started banging on the windscreen and roof of the car, demanding we wind our windows down. There were people everywhere as we were still within the confines of the circuit. The officers were very upset. They appeared to be off duty, as they were not carrying guns, but they were still policemen, and, as the head of communications for McLaren, my mind started spinning at 1,000mph. I imagined the two of us being hauled out of the car, cuffed, arrested for dangerous driving, and the whole thing ending up in the papers. Nightmare. Just picturing Ron Dennis's face was enough to prompt me to break out in a cold sweat.

By now both policemen were banging on the car, and one was gesturing that we had to get out of the Mercedes. I looked across at Senna, who was just staring ahead, as if all this had nothing to do with him. I wound my window down and told the policeman that, yes, we were going far too fast, and I was very sorry, but my friend, who was driving, did not feel very well and we were trying to get back to the hotel. The policeman leant into the car to see who the lunatic at the wheel was, recognised Senna, and got even angrier. Luckily his colleague decided to be lenient, and after a brief discussion across the roof of the car they let us go, with Mr Angry telling me in no uncertain terms not to be stupid again. All the while my Brazilian driver said nothing.

On we drove, only a little more sedately, to a small airport on the way to Heidelberg. We parked next to a private plane, and out Senna got, still without saying a word. He greeted the pilot, and into the plane they went. This was all very strange and I was wondering what was going on, but F1 teaches you to be patient. You get rather good at waiting around. Eventually he re-emerged, looked the plane up and down, and got on the telephone. He seemed to be talking to his father. Then he got back into the car and drove off. 'I'm thinking of buying it,' he explained for my benefit. Senna at his gruff best.

Mika Hakkinen, too, was something of an enigma in his early years. 'He was very quick, unbelievably fast,' recalled

Jo Ramirez. 'He really had natural speed. I don't think he was much of a test driver, though he got better and better. But the biggest problem with Mika was that he didn't have the consistency. He used to get tired during the race. Both mentally and physically, it seemed. I remember the one thing he used to say at the end of a race was "Please, don't push me." "Mika, you've got to push." But he'd get pissed off. "Please, don't push me!" And he knew that was his problem. In his first year at McLaren [1993], when he took over from Michael Andretti, at the Japanese GP he qualified only a few tenths behind Ayrton, who was on pole. Mika was third, and just by a few tenths, so he was quick. Come the race, he was 40 seconds behind. Mika finished third, a podium finish, and Ayrton won. Later, Mika said the car was fine, he had no problems at all, he just couldn't believe that he was almost a second a lap slower than Ayrton. But that's what it takes to be a champion. Schumacher could go and do 30 qualifying laps during the race if he needed to. He did it in Hungary once, when they changed the pit-stop strategy from two stops to three stops. I remember they said to him, "Do 25 laps like qualifying laps", and he said, "OK." Senna could do that, Stewart could have done that, but Mika just could not. That was his Achilles heel. But he did work on it and he got better and better. Mika was very good under pressure, though; he didn't make mistakes. That's another really good quality that Schumacher didn't have: he wasn't good under pressure. [Jim] Clark wasn't good under pressure either. He was a fantastic driver – so quick, so fast on his own, so quick at setting the pace – but the moment he had someone, especially somebody he recognised as good, he made mistakes.

'Everybody has their weak point, no matter how fantastic they are. I think the only weakness I can find in Senna is that he was not patient. He lost so many races through impatience. If he was behind someone, he was always trying to pass them. He became impatient and he didn't study the way he was going to pass them. Schumacher instead would stay behind and wait. Once he was behind Damon and waited a few laps to study the weaker points of Damon over the lap. It was in Portugal, and Damon was braking too early at the Corkscrew, so after two laps Schumacher tried to get closer and closer to him, and on the third attempt he got through. Senna did that sometimes, but not always. But he had to do it to pass someone who was a top driver, like Prost. In Phoenix there was an undulation in the road; everybody changed over to the other side because the car jumped. For a couple of laps Ayrton went on the undulating part of the track to see how bad it was, and, yes, the car was jumping, but it wasn't losing that much speed. So he went up behind Prost and the Frenchman moved over a couple of times to stop him from overtaking and pushing him towards the undulation. Finally Senna decided to go for it. He jumped up, but he still managed to pass Prost. He told me later he felt so good about it, as he was sure Prost had wondered how he had managed to pass him.

'He always used to say that other drivers could be very quick, but the thing that made the difference was the split-second decision of where you're going to pass people. The same happened when he lost the Italian Grand Prix in 1988 because he was going to pass Jean-Louis Schlesser again – I think he already passed him once. Just before the chicane, three laps before the end, the Ferraris were catching up and he was right behind Schlesser and he decided to pass there and then. Schlesser, who was making his F1 debut at the age of 40 in place of Nigel Mansell, who was unwell, saw him in the mirror and just braked too late. He went off in the chicane, on to the grass, and then came up and caught Ayrton on the way back. I asked him later, "Why didn't you wait?" But he was so impatient. The same thing happened in the Brazilian Grand Prix with the Japanese driver Satoru Nakajima: he went to pass him, so Nakajima moved to one side, but he did it too quickly, they spun, and they hit each other. He could have passed him after, but he was just too impatient.'

Ramirez also told the story of when Gerhard Berger took a pair of scissors to Ron Dennis's clothes. The two were famous for all kinds of pranks. 'You know how Ron is with his clothes,' Ramirez began. 'At every race, on Sunday mornings, he will have his luggage sent back to England, ahead of him. So, when he gets to the motor home he just has the clothes he's going to wear after the race – normally a brand-new shirt and trousers. Ron would wear a shirt five or six times, then get a new one. Well, once, Gerhard got some scissors from the kitchen and cut off the sleeves on the shirts and the legs on the trousers. When Ron came back from the pit wall after the race and discovered this he was really not pleased. He had to go home in his Marlboro overalls – the team's gear of course, which he hated. There were no limits to Gerhard's jokes.' Ramirez also mentioned Nelson Piquet, who was one of many drivers who had to pee at the end of each race. The mechanics even made a hole in the bottom of the chassis so that he could pee during the race. They used to hate to clean the car afterwards.

Nigel Mansell was a great driver who managed to put an awful lot of extra bums on seats during his time in F1. He became a popular hero in Britain, as big as any footballer around at the time. Someone once told me that he appealed especially to white males who wash their cars on Sunday mornings on their driveways. As if this was a bad thing. Bums are bums and seats are seats. Promoters now wish they had the crowds when he was about the place, winning races, wearing the Union Jack on his sleeve, bringing guts and passion to the circuits.

But it took a long time for the F1 establishment to accept him. His Brummie accent, his propensity to moan about all sorts of matters, even his physique – more sturdy yeoman than jockey – and the lack of what was considered a trophy wife were measured against him by a surprising number of people. By all accounts he was, like so many drivers, quite insecure and therefore defensive and hard to work with. He was followed everywhere by a substantial group of British journalists whose sole reason for being in the paddock was to report on 'Our Nige'. Nothing else mattered. I discovered this to my cost when, after filing a piece from the San Marino Grand Prix, I made a check call from Bologna airport before boarding the plane. I was passed from the sub-editor's desk to the sports editor's office. 'Norman,' he said, 'what happened to Our Nige? I can't see him in the first paragraph.' 'Well,' I replied, 'he retired early, so I wrote about him near the end of the piece.' 'What's the matter with you? We're a British paper. We *have* to lead on Mansell.' So the article was rewritten to accommodate the wishes of the sports editor.

All good column inches for Mansell, of course, but also this kind of treatment can build a momentum of its own, and not always a positive one. It was tough on him to have a whole nation behind him. It is one of the reasons why Enzo Ferrari favoured non-Italian drivers as he felt the pressure of driving a Ferrari would be too much for an Italian. To this day Ferrari are reluctant to hire top drivers from Italy, though the cupboard has been bare lately in that country. Mansell, of course, was a great success for them, but he had to wait 72 races before winning his first GP. Jenson Button has experienced similar pressures, partly relieved by his maiden F1 win in 2006.

But Mansell was a one-off. I remember being very pleased that the supposed 'insider' at my first Grand Prix who told me that Mansell was not the right man for the sport and that we needed more glamorous drivers turned out to be so spectacularly wrong. I often had breakfast with Mansell inside the garage, or in the motor home. He was early to the circuit, and it was a good time to just chat about all kinds of things. I always found him to be good company and a very correct, nearly old-fashioned sort of man. And he played a mean game of football. But he did keep a sting in the tail for me.

When McLaren took him on in 1995, the team was confronted with the fact that he was built quite differently to the 'average' driver and simply would not fit into the tub. It was all very embarrassing for everyone, and as the main team spokesman I had to field a number of difficult questions. The worst was a BBC *One o'Clock News* grilling conducted by the veteran broadcaster John Tusa, who included the Mansell-too-fat-for-F1 item as the funny of the programme. Ron Dennis was watching live upstairs in the McLaren offices while I was in the trophy room downstairs doing my best not to become a joke item for Mr Tusa and his producers. Mansell did drive that car, eventually, but he never got to grips with it and left soon after.

My long-lasting memory of him is his stunning win in Hungary in 1989, when he started twelfth and managed to pass so many on a circuit known for being nigh on impossible to overtake on. Ferrari fans called him 'Il Leone', the Lion, and next to Gilles Villeneuve he has a place in their hearts. But his iconic status with 'ordinary' folk was summed up for me as I was leaving the Hungaroring after the race. It was late and dark, and not many people seemed to be still camping out in the woods around the circuit. Yet I could hear a trumpet playing the Triumphal March from Giuseppe Verdi's *Aida*. It was a defining moment, and I realised how much Mansell's win meant to so many fans, people who had nothing to do with the glamour and razzmatazz of five-star hotels, private planes and fancy cars, and who cared even less about rule changes and the latest engineering gizmo. They simply liked good racing, they would pay good money to see it, and they would blow their trumpet in a dark Magyar forest to celebrate their happiness. Their man had won, and he had done it heroically. What more could anyone want?

Another driver who did not make it at McLaren, but for entirely different reasons, was Michael Andretti. It's always tough for a son to live up to a father's success, especially if he decides to operate in the same sport. Mario raced in all kinds of motor sport from 1961 to 2000, taking part in 879 races, winning 111 of them, and notching up 109 poles. That's a conversation-stopper around any dinner table – truly amazing stats. Within the stats there are sparkling cameos, like his 1993 Champ Car win in Phoenix when he was 53 years old. Or his Indy 500 and Daytona 500 wins. Or his Sebring 12 win. The list is very long and varied. He was F1 world champion too, in 1978, but he'd already had a few bites at F1. Indeed his first ever F1 race, at Watkins Glen, was a decade earlier. He qualified on pole. This ability to switch between different formula cars, then to stock cars and even into drag racing, truly sets him apart among modern drivers. Mario was also blessed with matinée idol good looks. In short, he was a pretty cool and talented guy all round. And a very hard act to follow.

Michael, his eldest son, started racing in 1980. He progressed through the ranks and in 1991 became Indy Car World Series champion. Two years later he was in F1, signed up to McLaren. There were high expectations. His team-mate was Ayrton Senna, and the team itself was strong: it had won the world title two years earlier and the same workforce was still in place. But the young American never really crossed over to F1. Whereas Mario devoured everything in his way, his son appeared to be a little more timid, and he found it hard to adapt to a non-American environment. To everyone's surprise he announced he would not live in Europe and would commute between races.

It was a strange time with Michael in the team. He wouldn't really know what to do with himself, especially if his wife was not with him. She tried hard, telling anyone who would listen that he was soon going to get his 'tiger eyes back', and then 'watch out everyone'. But the tiger never arrived and he didn't last the season. 'He did the Italian Grand Prix, but that was the last one,' Jo Ramirez recalled. 'He was supposed to be going out before that, but I think Mario said to Ron, "Please let him do that race." So he raced the Italian GP and he finished third – by far his best race. He got a podium, but then he was sent back home. He just never had the commitment, didn't really want to do it. When it came to it, Mario pushed him so much, as he wanted to relive his life through Michael, but it just didn't work.

'At the beginning Ron warmed to him. He believed that he could do it. But as races went by he changed his mind. He just didn't apply himself to driving a F1 car. And I remember that Ron offered him his house in France, and his plane, so he didn't have to go back to the States all the time. Michael used to go back and forth in Concorde, and it just didn't work. When he left he said, "I didn't have enough opportunities to test." Bullshit. Can you imagine what any driver in the world would give to be able to drive a McLaren next to Senna? I mean, what an opportunity! To be part of McLaren, to live nearby, to go testing every time McLaren was testing, and to really concentrate that year at 150 per cent, whether he wanted to do it or not. One year of his life – that's nothing. What an opportunity wasted. I think if his father had been a carpenter, he would have been a carpenter. He had a very cushy life in the States and he wasn't prepared to change it. He had no interest whatsoever in driving Formula One. It was such a waste, because we could have had Mika from the beginning of the year.'

He certainly seemed to be way out of his depth, and his social skills then were not likely to endear him to Ron Dennis. One day I was sitting with Ron in the back of the motor home. It was quite a small area, pretty much devoted to a semi-circular sofa and a table. You had to squeeze round and under the fixed table in order to sit on the sofa. I was briefing Dennis about something to do with the media when the pneumatic door opened, and there stood Michael Andretti, shy smile on his face. 'Hey, you guys ...' He walked in, pushed past and over me, and sat between me and Dennis. It's a silly thing, but F1 is very hierarchical and secretive. All motor homes have an inner sanctum, and one does not just walk in and sit down if the team boss is there in conversation. It was a faux pas, but of course Michael, coming from a much more relaxed American environment, and not possessing great social intelligence anyway, seemed completely oblivious to it all. Dennis just stared at him. Eventually he asked, 'Can I help you?' If words could be described as frozen, well, these were. But Michael was still unconcerned and replied, 'No, man, just chilling out.' You had to be there; it was something to behold. The super-tight Ron Dennis being told by his failing driver – who in his boss's view should have been locked away in a room with engineers buried in data sheets in an effort to find some speed – that he was just 'chilling out' was a priceless moment. To this day I wonder if Dennis knew what 'chilling out' meant. It was certainly not a phrase bandied about the shop floor in Woking.

I can recall another incident that illustrated the gulf between Michael and the rest of the drivers. Normally top drivers and team owners find a smart way out of the Spa circuit in Belgium – no mixing with the great unwashed for them. Helicopters and police escorts are the most common form of fast exit, but that's not possible everywhere, and Spa is one of those difficult areas where the brilliant Belgian police yearly devise new ways of stopping cars and drivers from going north to Brussels and its airport; they like sending everyone south. So there is much poring over maps and then everyone drives very fast – hire cars; who cares? – towards the airport. I was in one such car, in the back seat, together with one of the senior engineers at McLaren and Mrs Dennis. Michael was at the steering wheel and we were waiting for Ron Dennis. When he eventually arrived, he leant into the car to see who was driving. When he spotted Michael, he told him to get out, that he was going to drive instead. Now that, for a racing driver, is just about as low as you can get. Getting turfed out of the driving seat by your middle-aged F1 boss must have been awful for him.

Talking of the great unwashed, some years later I was in Shanghai, on the eve of the first ever Grand Prix there. I was helping with the organisation of the race, and, as part of a raft of media initiatives, we facilitated a number of trips for the drivers across the city, taking in spots as varied as the sixteenth-century Yuyuan Gardens and its tea houses, as well as the Pearl Tower in the very modern district of Pudong, across the Huangpu River. I was with Giancarlo Fisichella and Felipe Massa, then Sauber drivers, and it was refreshing to see how neither minded at all crossing the river in a standard passenger ferry, as opposed to the private launch that had been arranged but which had not arrived. Everybody was very worried they would throw a wobbly about having to share a boat with ordinary Shanghai folk from all walks of life, and some of their livestock too, but both drivers were as good as gold. Indeed they clearly enjoyed themselves.

Later, we finished off the short tour on the terrace of one of the new ritzy restaurants on the Bund. They enjoyed a glass of wine – indeed Fisichella more than one as he tried the different bottles on offer – and the talk was about the wine, and football. It was a very pleasant time spent with drivers who were not self-important, and who could get into the spirit of a media activity without acting up and making life hard for anyone associated with it. Both laughed a lot, especially when I asked Fisichella whether he had done many computer-simulated laps of the new circuit. No one had driven round it yet, but a number of teams had bought satellite time so as to get a good view of the circuit, and then built computer models to establish parameters for car set-up, fuel consumption and so on. The Italian looked at me over his glass of wine, looked at his team-mate, and said, 'Are you crazy? This is Sauber we are driving for. Computer simulation?' And the laughter continued. On race day they did very well, finishing seventh and eighth ahead of one McLaren, one Ferrari and one Williams, all teams that would have spent a fortune on satellite time and computer simulation. In this case, laughter, a glass of wine and sheer good driving were the right formula. It probably is most of the time. It certainly was not so long ago.

One who would have approved of this approach to driving is Eddie Irvine, famous for getting into a fight with Ayrton Senna and chasing skirt across all continents. He was very good for the sport as he injected some much-needed dashing derring-do and rebel spirit when most other drivers were being neutered by sponsors and media managers. The fight wasn't a fight, by the way, more of a tipsy lunge from the Brazilian, who had been given a glass or two by the mischievous Gerhard Berger. When Senna walked out of the prefab motor home in Suzuka – it's not all glamour in F1; there is a little rough with the smooth – his race engineer Giorgio Ascanelli followed him out and motioned for me to come too. By the time we caught up with Senna he was already walking into the Jordan prefab. (As you may recall, during this 1993 Japanese GP the Brazilian overtook the first-race rookie Irishman, who immediately dived back past him. He suggested later that the multiple world champion was driving too slowly.) Senna quickly spotted Irvine, who was sitting on a table dangling his legs. He went straight up to him and immediately started talking about 'respect' and 'seniority' to the uppity Irish driver, who refused to back down, saying that he drove his own race and it was up to his rivals to overtake him, if they could. Seeing that Irvine was not going to apologise, and that words were not going to get him anywhere, Senna lost his cool and sort of half-lunged towards Irvine, then lost his balance as he went forwards. Irvine half-fell off the table, and the general commotion made it all look a lot more than it was. By then I had my arms around Senna and was pulling him away, and Ascanelli had interposed his large frame between the two drivers as Irvine was now beginning to look as if he would throw a punch. We then walked Senna back to our motor home. Of course it made news, and Eddie Jordan, always one with an eye to publicity, revved the story up as much as he could.

Irvine settled in at Ferrari and enjoyed life to the full in Italy. His career was overshadowed by being Michael Schumacher's team-mate – he was very much number two in the pecking order – but he had his chance to shine in 1999 when Schumacher broke his leg at Silverstone. It didn't quite work out for him, but he still walked away in the end with a substantial property portfolio and a prominent place on *Forbes*'s Rich List.

And he was one hell of a fast driver. Every year Marlboro organise a get-together for the Italian media in Madonna di Campiglio, an upmarket ski resort in the Dolomites. The Ferrari drivers are also invited. It's a way of starting off the season with lots of positive column inches in the local media. One year I was there. Eddie Irvine was due to come, but he had been delayed on his way from a test and had landed at Bologna airport late. From there to Campiglio is normally a three-hour drive, and the last 60 kilometres are on twisty mountain roads. The organisers of the dinner really wanted Irvine to be there, so they were trying to stay in touch by mobile telephone. It didn't take long for them to start looking a little surprised: he was making very good progress in his Alfa on the motorway. One of the organisers, who had done much hillclimbing and knew the local roads very well, warned that he would have to slow down once he left the motorway as there was quite a lot of traffic and overtaking was not an option most of the time. Besides, it seemed Irvine had a lady passenger, so he would have to watch himself.

As Irvine progressed up the mountain roads, once or twice asking for directions, the gathered guests and media were periodically relayed his position, which always appeared to be a lot further up the mountain than anyone had imagined. He was clearly flying, and they just loved him for it. There he was, a Ferrari driver, in an Alfa Romeo, taming mountain and car to his will, with a lady beside him. When he entered the restaurant, the lady at his side, having knocked an hour off the driving time, he received a standing ovation, and his name was chanted football-style. For red-blooded Italians, this was cool. This is why they loved Gilles Villeneuve and Nigel Mansell. Passion and derring-do, and a little madness. The spirit of Ferrari embodied in a driver.

As I said at the beginning of this chapter, many of these snapshots feature the great Ayrton Senna. To me he was the most complex and complete champion of my era. He was generous and approachable too, once the first barriers had been taken away. Professor Sid Watkins once told me about the time Senna had given to support some of the Prof's charities in Scotland. No fanfare, no media managers; he would just turn up alongside the Prof, at a school or wherever, and talk to people, help out, be there. And, as many have pointed out in these pages, he was the first to bring a sense of professionalism to the sport. James Hunt was a man's man and a lady's man. Charming, wonderfully talented, a natural. As were his contemporaries. Driving was fun, dashing, and dangerous. Senna took matters to a different level.

In my first year working at McLaren, 1993, the BBC were filming a seven-part documentary series called *The Team: A Season With McLaren*. I was very involved as Ron Dennis had asked me in the first place what I thought of the project, which was originally going to be a race-by-race documentary focusing on both McLaren and Benetton. At the time I was still working for the *Sunday Times*, so I was able to offer an objective opinion. I told Dennis that McLaren would be murdered on screen: the grey British traditional racing team pitted against the colourful upstarts from Italy, with girls and fashion and Flavio Briatore. It was a non-contest, and I suspected it had been set up this way. I suggested doing just McLaren and booting out Benetton. But, I warned, the BBC would want greater access to the team. It would really have to be an 'as live' documentary, and it would be a first for an F1 team, where secrecy is key to everything that is done. The BBC went for it and commissioned six episodes, and Dennis asked me to view all the rough material so that we could control the output. There were quite a few ups and downs as the BBC and Dennis wrestled over what could be shown, and over the meaning of the word 'control', but in the end the BBC liked the material so much they commissioned a final episode, which conveniently dovetailed with the last GP of the year, in Australia.

It was Senna's last race for the team before he left for Williams and, as luck would have it, he won. Emotions were very high. The BBC cameras were quite intrusive – it was their job to be – so Dennis, an instinctively shy man, was forever finding dark corners to hide in. This time, when the race was over, it was at the back of the garage, among the freight boxes. He was standing there with a senior figure from Cortaulds, one of our long-time sponsors, a big South African bear of a man. He was crying his eyes out, as was Dennis. It was all about Senna, about him winning in a car everyone knew was a bad one, about him leaving the team, about the inability to keep him at McLaren. It was a release after a tough year. As these things are often contagious, I started crying too. So there we were: three grown men, crying together, hidden at the back of a garage, while outside everyone was celebrating.

This is why everyone who works in this sport loves it. Emotions are always very near the surface, no matter how tough everyone makes out they are.

These have been snapshots of my time so far in and around F1. There are more, which for reasons of politeness and discretion I ought not to share, but I hope those that have made it on to the page here have given a glimpse of how drivers tick in their working lives. My final snapshot is of Juan Manuel Fangio. In the summer of 1992, soon after the Brazilian GP, I arranged to interview him in Buenos Aires, where he had an office in the Mercedes HQ. He was 81 at the time. He stood up to greet me, a dapper man in a sober grey suit and tie, lively eyes, firm handshake. Andy Priaulx talked about special drivers having an aura around them. Well, Fangio's was tangible, even while wearing a suit in an office.

He invited me to sit down. We established that we could speak in Italian, and before I could say anything at all he complimented me on my work. I was thrown by this, and, for a few seconds, I looked at him uncomprehendingly. He enjoyed this moment, then with a little smile he turned his head to look at a side table I hadn't seen, on which were loads of copies of the *Sunday Times* and other publications I had written for. He then tapped a pile of papers in front of him and said, 'I have read them all. They have been translated for me. Now, I don't really agree on what you say about Senna ...' And off he went, speaking beautifully about driving, timing, attitude. I was truly taken aback, by his attention to detail, but mostly by his professionalism in wanting to make a judgement on the person he was going to be interviewed by. It was a form of respect I found humbling, and to this day I count that encounter as the most thrilling interview I have ever done.

To my great disappointment and regret I was unable to take up his subsequent invitation to join him at his motor museum in his home town of Balcarce. He was flying down the next day in a Mercedes private aeroplane; would I care to join him? Alas, a house-buying emergency back in London needed to be attended to. I just had to leave Buenos Aires that night. I never managed to meet him again, and he passed away a few years later, in 1995. But one day I will make my way to Balcarce. I promised Juan Manuel Fangio I would.

CONCLUSION

I have met quite a few drivers. I've worked with some and interviewed others, though I've never tried to get too close to any of them. They are usually pretty focused when at the races, and I have always disliked the sycophantic way some people have with them. As has already been pointed out in this book, the very qualities that turn them into such special individuals are also the ones that make them relatively hard to get on with in terms of normal interaction. They do talk a lot, or maybe listen, to their engineers; they also talk to their team owners; they talk less to their mechanics (though there are a few notable exceptions) and as little as they can get away with to the media and the sponsors; and in public they try to be as anodyne as possible, blank-faced whenever they go from motor home to pits, or to the car park to their car. The sight of Kimi Raikkonen with a cigar clamped in his mouth and a bottle of beer in each hand is literally that – quite a sight. But this was Shanghai in 2005 and the young Finn was having fun at the end-of-season party. Good for him, too, after a season of mind-numbingly low-voiced mumbles where the words 'tyre', 'set-up' and maybe 'wet' might just stand out. There is a personality in there somewhere, but modern F1 tends to frown on any uncontrolled expression of soul.

Bernie Ecclestone has done more than anyone else to turn a sport where a bunch of gentlemen from the UK, Germany and Italy battled it out on track by day and had the very best time possible at all other times, into the hard-nosed, commercially driven affair it is today. But he too laments the passing of fun. 'Today, it doesn't seem, at least driver-wise, that you have the characters we used to have,' he said. 'I don't know why it is, whether they're under too much pressure or whether they're earning too much money. They have to behave now. James Hunt today would never be tolerated by Marlboro the way he was when he was driving for them. They are looking for a different image. I don't think they are even right. If I were a sponsor I'd rather have a character than just another guy who pitches up and says thank you to the sponsors, thanks to the engine company, thanks to the tyre manufacturers. You don't need that, you need someone who is a bit of a character.'

This is probably why Ecclestone had a soft spot for Jacques Villeneuve, the grunge-chic son of the legendary Gilles. With his shirt joyously untucked, his John Lennon glasses and an indefinable air of cool about him, he was the one who could have appealed to the younger audience the sport needs. And if he didn't really misbehave at all, it's because he was a dedicated racing professional, albeit with other interests in his life – like music, for example. Otherwise what we have is largely a uniform body of young men who just do as they are told by their handlers, while the older ones have become smooth and professionally slippery when required to speak. The exceptions seem to be the very young Sebastian Vettel and Robert Kubica, who seem to have the confidence to be able to joke and fence with the media, to be irreverent. 'He's my hero, but the cars will still drive around in circles,' said Vettel when asked what he thought the future of F1 would be like after Michael Schumacher's retirement. 'You could run through the paddock stark naked and nobody would notice,' he commented as everyone in Monza was awaiting news of Schumacher's retirement. 'Maybe I shouldn't be a Formula One driver at all – I don't look like one' was Kubica's great line at the FIA press conference in Shanghai in 2006.

In the end, though, driving is not about looking cool in the paddock, or being able to trade clever phrases with the press pack. It's about winning, and much more, some of it still indefinable, which is still part of what makes these men so unique. When I covered my first Grand Prix, in San Marino in 1989, unable to write anything in any way trenchant or with any kind of gravitas – I was so conscious of knowing so little about the sport – I tried to look at it all with different eyes. I was struck by how one of the reasons for the great appeal of the sport was that the drivers were very much like medieval jousting knights: they wore colours, a loyal retinue prepared their steed, a master of arms discussed fighting tactics with them, and so on. And the public were fascinated because these men were going out to do what they could never bring themselves to do. It was, after all, very dangerous; it could even get you killed. Best to watch from a comfortable seat.

The aloofness of the drivers struck me as so different from many other sportsmen I had witnessed as a sports writer. All were hustling and bustling around them, but they were always in their own world as they donned balaclava, then helmet, then slipped into the car, and into their 'zone'. Granted, as many have said in these pages, that all top sportspeople share some of the gifts that make them supreme competitiors, but I still feel that drivers are particularly special. In terms of loneliness, danger and speed, I suppose a downhill skier is the closest to them. But their race is much shorter. No less of an achievement, of course, but less concentration time is required, and skis, so far at least, don't require constant electronic setting and fuel adjusting throughout the race. Team players, especially in the top sports, must withstand in some way even greater pressure as the heavy hand of the media is even more present than it is in F1. A blunder in goal, a dropped pass in front of the try line, a fumbled catch in a Test – such things can turn the world into a very lonely place for the unfortunate player. But teams stick together and there will be immediate support for the player on the pitch and in the changing rooms. Drivers do not have that instant camaraderie on tap. It may sound ironic, but the flight back in the private jet can be a very lonely trip. Luxury is not a stick-on plaster for the pain and hurt.

As I walked past the business side of the pits at Imola all those years ago, the one open to the track, the knights in shining armour were busily getting ready, driving out and back in, and the garages were bristling with tension, expectation and professionalism. It was a wonderful spectacle, the movement, the colours, the sponsors' logos and the faces all blending together. A happy scene, too, one that any visitor could have enjoyed, even if they didn't know too much about the business of driving and winning. I filed a piece along these lines, very upbeat, and, as I was working for a Sunday paper, I had the whole of race day to wander about and soak up the crowd and the magic of F1.

A few hours later Gerhard Berger's car burst into flames as he hit the wall at Tamburello, near where his great friend Ayrton Senna would lose his life a few years later. That's when I realised that, as in medieval jousting, despite all the precautions, the knights could get hurt. The colours, noise and the fun surrounding it all could easily turn into darkness. Reading about it, or seeing it on the television, is not the same. Live, you experience the awful silence of the crowd. People's eyes look so different, as does their body language. In some ways it is as if everyone goes into collective shock. All except for the medical teams, and the racing teams too, already planning how to cope, to re-deploy, to carry on. It's a dangerous business, and it still is, despite all the safety innovations.

Max Mosley chose as his stand-out drivers of all time men who were 'racers' racers' – a wonderfully resonant alliterative phrase that for me captures the magic these men perform every couple of weeks for our enjoyment.

INDEX

accidents 52-53, 56-57, 63, 97, 114-116,
117, 153-167, 185, 211, 213, 214, 251
medical assessment of driver
160-163
Adelaide 114-115
Aguri Suzuki F1 team 27
Albers, Christijan 95, 149
Alesi, Jean 88, 91-92, 94, 198-199
Allen, James 48-50, 51, 73-74, 79
Alonso, Fernando 21, 26, 30, 50, 55,
79-80, 81, 83, 173, 175, 180, 183,
200, 201, 204, 209
and Flavio Briatore 45, 107, 108
move to McLaren 26, 106, 193,
194, 201
Amon, Chris 207
Andretti, Mario 234, 235
Andretti, Michael 193-194, 228,
234-237
Armstrong, Lance 45, 147
arrogance, drivers' 74, 79-80
Arrows F1 team 107, 197
Ascanelli, Giorgio 59-60, 67, 75, 239,
240
Ascari, Alberto 217
aura, drivers' 172, 178, 244
Australian GP 114-115, 194, 243
Austria 210
Autosport 19, 86, 90, 191

'bag carriers' 70-71, 76, 121
Balcarce 245
Barcelona 135-136, 141
Barilla, Paolo 98, 99, 100-101
Barilla family 98-99
Barnard, John 202
Barnes, Simon 50
Barrichello, Rubens 93, 96, 166
BBC TV programmes 154, 233,
242-243
Beckham, David 25, 26, 44
Belgian GP 86, 88, 134, 162,
217-218
Benetton 31-32, 190, 199-200
Benetton, Luciano 33
Benetton F1 team 32, 33, 69, 88-89, 90,
91, 99, 138, 148, 199, 201, 242
Benetton family 199
Berger, Gerhard 70, 88, 132, 155, 164,
181, 183, 191, 230-231, 239, 251
Best, George 44

Blash, Herbie 89
Blundell, Mark 105-106, 110
BMW 19, 26, 34, 190
F1 team 34, 71, 108, 129, 190, 191
World Touring Car Championship
69-70, 187
Boutsen, Thierry 79
Brabham, Jack 213, 217
Brabham F1 team 89, 189
Bradshaw, Anne 54, 71, 75, 76, 77
Brambilla, Vittorio 205
Brawn, Ross 47, 69
Brazilian GP 134-135, 146, 204,
207, 230
Briatore, Flavio 31-32, 45-46, 55, 101,
103, 107-108, 184, 191, 199-201, 242
at Benetton 88-89, 90, 91, 190
at Renault 18, 93, 95, 190, 202
Brundle, Martin 73-74, 105, 108-111,
117
Buenos Aires 244-245
Button, Jenson 93, 108, 109, 200-201,
232

Camel 108
car reliability 81
car set-up 61
Chrysler 224
circuit knowledge 83-84
Clark, Jim 40, 52, 56, 81, 228-229
Coaker, Graham 205
communicating with team 59-60,
61-62, 63-65, 67-69, 70-71, 72, 112,
174, 216
Concorde Agreement 91, 206
constructors 189, 190-191
Convey, Gerry 146
Cosworth Ford engine 89, 189, 223
Coton, Didier 28-30, 46, 54-55, 111-
114, 115-117, 118-119, 120, 122
Coulthard, David 19, 39, 109, 110,
180, 183, 194, 211
courage 55-56
Courage, Piers 205
Courtaulds 243

danger 51, 52, 54-55
de Angelis, Elio 96, 166
De Cesaris, Andrea 28
deaths 51, 53, 155 see also Senna,
Ayrton: death

Dennis, Ron 22-23, 25, 31, 38, 108, 184, 189, 190-194, 197, 230, 233, 242, 243
  and Ayrton Senna 156, 167, 221-222, 224, 225, 227
  and Michael Andretti 235, 236-237
Dernie, Frank 47, 62-65, 67-68, 69, 70, 71, 72, 76
diet 129, 132, 144, 179
Diniz, Pedro 96, 97, 198
Donnelly, Martin 156, 157
Doohan, Mick 78
Doornbos, Robert 65-66, 80-81, 92
DTM (Deutschen Tourenwagen Masters) series 28-29, 138, 149

Earnhardt Jr, Dale 25
Ecclestone, Bernie 25, 32, 85, 89, 90-91, 93, 159, 190, 200, 204, 205, 247-248
Edwards, Martin 26
Elf Pilotage 108-109
Elizabeth II, HRH Queen 25
engine manufacturers 190
engineers, race 57, 63
  drivers' relationship 59-60, 61-62, 63-65, 67-69, 70-71, 72, 75-76, 82-83, 112, 121, 174, 216
entertainment 31, 32-33
extroverts 62-63

F1 Racing 206
F1-Racing (Japan) 27
Fangio, Juan Manuel 51, 81, 185-186, 217, 244-245
fear 53, 54-55, 57, 184-185, 186, 213-215
Ferrari, Enzo 232
Ferrari F1 team 19, 81, 189, 192, 232, 240, 241
FIA (Fédération International de l'Automobile) 27, 33, 205, 210, 249
  medical emergency team 157-158, 160
Firman, Ralph 199
Fisichella, Giancarlo 45, 107, 108, 199, 238-239
fitness, physical 95, 123-151 see also training
  circuits 134-136
  heat, dealing with 127, 135, 145
fitness coaches 128-130
fluid intake 127, 136, 144, 145
food intake 129, 132, 144, 179

football 30, 44, 136-137
Forbes Top Ten Sports Rich List 25, 240
Formula 2: 212-213
Formula 3: 73-74, 107, 109, 130, 172
Formula BMW 26, 34
Formula Nippon 27
Formula One Management (FOM) 18, 33
Foster, Trevor 87
Frentzen, Heinz-Harald 87
Fry, Nick 191

G-forces 125-126, 138, 139, 140, 142, 143, 150
Gachot, Bertrand 85, 86, 87
girlfriends 76
GP2 26, 103
Guardian 26

Hakkinen, Mika 28-29, 37, 38-39, 119, 120, 132, 138, 191, 194, 209, 227-228
  accident 114-116
  early career 59-60, 63
Hallam, Steve 67
Hamilton, Lewis 24-25, 26, 93, 192, 193, 194
HANS device 52, 158-159, 214
Harstein, Gary 124-128, 158, 159-164
Hawthorn, Mike 213
Head, Patrick 47, 137
Heidfeld, Nick 54, 129, 132, 161, 163
Herbert, Johnny 91-92, 148-150, 151
Herd, Robin 205
Hill, Damon 29, 53, 195, 197-198, 229
Hill, Graham 52
Hockenheim 226-227
Honda 34, 190, 222, 223
  F1 team 34, 93, 190, 191
Horner, Christian 191, 202-203
Hungarian GP 135, 198, 228, 233-234
Hunt, James 28, 54, 124, 138, 150-151, 242, 248

Ickx, Jacky 39
Ide, Yuji 27-28
Ilmor 87
Imola 155, 164-165, 166-167, 249-251
income 25-26
information, drivers processing 43-44, 127-128
injuries 130, 143, 160, 161-162
Interlagos 134-135, 146, 204
introverts 62, 63, 72

Irvine, Eddie 25, 94, 239-240, 241
Italian GP 88, 102, 230, 235
ITV 48, 49, 73

Japanese GP 135, 228, 239-240
Jenkinson, Denis 222
Jerez 156, 194
jockeys 123-124
Jones, Alan 68
Jordan, Eddie 85-87, 89, 90, 91-92,
    102, 103, 191, 198-199, 203, 240
Jordan Grand Prix F1 team 85,
    86-87, 88, 89, 91, 92, 107, 148, 189

Karthikeyan, Narain 92, 149
karting 210
Klien, Christian 96
Kolles, Colin 102
Kovalainen, Heikki 45, 108, 202
Kristensen, Tomas 106
Kubica, Robert 54, 93, 129, 248, 249

Lamborghini 224
Lammers, Jan 97
Lauda, Niki 52, 81, 206, 219
Le Mans 24-Hour race 79, 99, 105,
    106, 138, 139, 140, 144
Leberer, Joseph 128-134, 135-136,
    137-138, 139, 142, 146, 151
Ligier F1 team 189
Liuzzi, Tonio 92
Lola F1 team 138

Macau 87, 169, 173, 178, 187
Madonna di Campiglio 240-241
Malaysian GP 135, 196
managers, drivers' 28-29, 33-34, 101,
    103, 105-122
Mansell, Nigel 49, 53, 72-73, 81, 83,
    88, 136-137, 148, 172, 173, 182,
    230, 231-234, 241
March 701 F1 car 218-219
March Engineering 205
Marlboro 28, 108, 189, 240-241,
    248
Martin, Neil 57
Mass, Jochen 87
Massa, Felipe 238
Matthews, Stanley 44
McLaren F1 team 22-23, 26, 59, 67,
    120, 138, 142, 146, 165, 183, 189,
    190, 192-194
    and Ayrton Senna 60, 74, 167,
    194, 197, 221-222, 224-226

Fernando Alonso's move to 26,
    106, 193, 194
Ford-engined car 42, 223
and Lewis Hamilton 26, 93
and Michael Andretti 234-237
and Mika Hakkinen 37, 38, 59,
    114-115, 116, 120, 191, 194, 228
and Nigel Mansell 136, 233
Technical Centre 18-19
TV documentary 242-243
McLaren-Honda F1 team 81, 138
McNally, Paddy 25
McNish, Allan 138-146
media relations 20-23, 71
medical assessment of driver after
    accident 160-163
medical facilities at circuits 159-160,
    161-162
mental strength, driver's 76-78, 79,
    175
Mercedes 81, 87-88, 149, 190, 191,
    226-227
    Junior Team 86-87, 88
Midland F1 86, 92, 102, 148-149, 196
    see also Spyker F1
Minardi, Giancarlo 99, 191
Minardi F1 team 66, 99, 107, 189, 199
Monaco GP 135, 143, 185-186, 207,
    217, 218
Monteiro, Tiago 92, 95, 149
Montoya, Juan Pablo 19-20, 23, 54,
    55-56, 72, 146, 147, 192, 204
Monza 88, 90, 102, 212-213
Morbidelli, Gianni 99
Mosley, Max 33, 158, 159, 190,
    205-219, 251
Moss, Sir Stirling 185-186, 217, 222

Nakajima, Saturo 230
Nannini, Alessandro 99
Neal, Anne 79
Neerpasch, Jochen 87-88, 89
Newey, Adrian 197, 202
Nissany, Chanoch 199
Nürburgring 83-84, 178
Nuvolari, Tazio 81

Paddock Club 22
Panis, Olivier 109
parents, drivers' 76
Patrese, Riccardo 216
Paul Stewart Racing 23-24
paying drivers 85-103
Pelé 44

Penske 97
Peterson, Ronnie 40, 205, 217, 218-219
Peugeot engine 224
Phillips, Ian 86-88, 89-92, 93-96, 101-103, 108, 120-121, 122, 128, 196
Phoenix 229
physical stresses 125-128
Piquet, Nelson 52, 77, 88, 231
Piquet Jr, Nelson 77
Portuguese GP 229
positive energy 173
pressure on drivers 50-51
Priaulx, Andy 69-70, 81-82, 169-187, 244
Prost, Alain 40-41, 52, 81, 88, 132, 149-150, 151, 165-166, 195, 206, 225, 229

qualities, driver's 30-31
Queanbeyan 79

race preparation 80-81
race starts 80
Racing Driver (1959) 222
Radio Montecarlo 20
radio transmissions 68-69
RAI (TV station) 155
Raikkonen, Kimi 23, 56, 108, 109, 146, 183, 184, 192, 209, 247
Ramirez, Jo 37-39, 40-41, 57, 164-167, 194, 197-198, 199, 202, 227-231, 235-236
  and drivers' courage 55, 56-57
  and pay drivers 96-98
Ratzenberger, Roland 53, 155, 166
reactions, drivers' 43-44, 128, 182
Real Madrid 108
Rebaque, Hector 96-97
Red Bull Racing F1 team 19, 20, 32, 34, 66, 96, 107, 109, 183, 191, 201, 202
Red Bulletin 60-62, 66, 191
Rees, Alan 205
relationship with team 59-60, 61-62, 63-65, 67-69, 70-71, 72, 75-76, 82-83, 121
Renault 18, 34, 109
  F1 team 93, 95, 107, 138-139, 200, 201-202
Richards, Dave 25
Rindt, Jochen 40, 76, 212-213, 217, 218
Rindt, Nina 76
Robertson, David and Steve 109
Rocky Mountains, Colorado 147

Rodriguez, Ricardo 38
Rosberg, Keke 28, 40, 77, 86, 94, 119-120, 196
Rosberg, Nico 77, 94, 195, 196
Rowlinson, Anthony 191-192, 193, 195-196, 200, 201, 203, 204
RTL (TV station) 91

safety 51-53, 210-213
safety innovations 158 see also HANS device
San Marino GP 155, 164-165, 166-167, 249-251
Sauber, Peter 191
Sauber F1 team 87, 108, 238, 239
Scheckter, Jody 39
Schlesser, Jean-Louis 230
Schumacher, Michael 29, 81, 128, 170, 175, 180, 182, 185, 207, 209, 217, 219, 240
  ability to adapt 44-45
  accidents 52, 53, 56
  arrogance 79
  aura 172
  with Benetton 69, 88-90
  car fire 160
  earnings 25
  fans 173
  fitness 124, 131, 134
  and Flavio Briatore 45, 107, 108, 200
  football games 30
  Hungarian GP 198, 228
  with Jordan 85, 86-87, 88, 199
  meditation 174, 179
  patience 229
  press officer 71
  retirement 248-249
  team motivation 215
  teamwork 83
  and Williams F1 car 166
Schumacher, Ralf 25, 72, 161
Senna, Ayrton 38, 42, 52, 57, 60, 73, 81, 88, 129, 177, 178, 195, 198, 217, 219, 223-227
  and Alain Prost 40-41
  arrogance 74, 79
  Australian GP (1993) 243
  courage 56
  death 53, 115, 155-156, 164-165, 166-167, 251
  and Eddie Irvine 239-240
  fears 53
  fitness 132, 133, 141, 149-150

in Formula Ford 172
generosity 242
impatience 229-230
Japanese GP (1993) 228
at McLaren 60, 74-75, 167, 194,
  197, 221-222, 224-226
and Professor Sid Watkins 158
and race engineer 67
religion 176, 221, 225
sponsorship 98
teamwork 82-83
and Williams F1 car 165, 166
Shanghai 238-239, 247, 249
Silverstone 59, 67-68, 87, 88, 102, 218,
  240
Simeno, Ricardo 97
Simtek Research 206
skiing 210
skills required, drivers' 23-24
Sordo, Stefano 60-62, 65
Spa-Francorchamps 86, 88, 99-101,
  134, 162, 237
Spanish GP 135-136, 156, 194
speed 34, 37, 38-39, 42-43, 45-48,
  49-50, 57, 58, 206
Speed, Scott 60, 62
sponsors 24, 92, 97, 98, 102, 106, 170,
  172, 189-190
Spyker F1 86, 95-96, 102 see also
  Midland F1
Stewart, Sir Jackie 17-18, 19, 23-24,
  25, 37, 50, 57, 81, 100, 186, 205, 208,
  215, 228
  and accidents 52-53, 56
  challenge of the car 41-42
  drivers and speed 40, 42-44, 128
  Nurburgring win 83-84
Stewart F1 team 148
Stoddart, Paul 107, 108
Sunday Times 100, 154, 198, 242, 244
  Rich List 25
Suzuka 135, 138-139, 239-240
Suzuki, Aguri 27
'switching off', drivers' 29-30
Symonds, Pat 201

team, communicating and
  relationship with 59-60, 61-62,
  63-65, 67-69, 70-71, 72, 75-76,
  82-83, 112, 121, 174, 216
team bosses 189-204
Theissen, Mario 34, 191
Thruxton 103
Toleman F1 team 190, 201

Toro Rosso, Scuderia 60, 191
Tour de France 147, 151
Toyota 34, 109, 190
  F1 team 34, 138, 190
training 130, 131, 133, 136-137, 139,
  140, 145-146, 147, 151, 182
Trulli, Jarno 45, 107, 108, 199, 200
Tusa, John 233
Tyrrell, Ken 37, 39, 190
Tyrrell F1 team 189

Unipart 172
United States GP 229, 234

Verstappen, Jos 97
Vettel, Sebastian 54, 108, 110, 248-249
Villeneuve, Gilles 20, 233, 241, 248
Villeneuve, Jacques 20-21, 29, 46-47,
  204, 248

Walker, Murray 48
Walkinshaw, Tom 107
Warwick, Derek 86
Watkins Glen 234
Watkins, Professor Sid 124, 156, 157,
  158, 159, 162, 242
Waugh, Steve 78
Webber, Mark 21-22, 45, 58, 75, 77-79,
  82, 106-107, 108, 134, 147-148, 201
  children's charity (Mark Webber
  Challenge) 30, 147-148
  father 78
Weber, Willy 89, 101
Wendlinger, Karl 87
Whitmarsh, Martin 203
Williams, Sir Frank 25, 31, 81, 94, 99,
  137, 147, 190, 191, 195-196, 203, 204
Williams Grand Prix Engineering F1
  team 81, 94, 107, 146, 157, 164, 165-
  166, 189,   190, 195, 196-
  197, 201, 205
wives 76
Woods, Tiger 24, 25, 45, 171
World Touring Car Championship
  69-70, 169, 173, 174, 178, 186-187
Wurz, Alex 195

Yamaha engine 89, 91
Yoong, Alex 199
young driver programmes 108-109

Zanardi, Alex 34
Zanarini, Enrico 101
Zolder 217-218